HONEST MOTHERHOOD

"A parenting book which focuses on the mother's needs as much as the child's! This no-judgement approach to gentle parenting will support families from pregnancy through toddlerhood and beyond. An amazing guide for caregivers who want to connect intimately with their child without neglecting their own wellbeing."

Amy Molloy
Author of *The World is a Nice Place*

HONEST
MOTHERHOOD

Words of comfort and musings into motherhood

Nikki Smith

radiate

radiate

Radiate Publishing
Melbourne, Australia.

www.radiatepublishing.com.au
www.facebook.com/radiatepublishing
enquiries@radiatepublishing.com.au

First published by Radiate Publishing 2021
Design and typography © Radiate Publishing 2021
Text © Nikki Smith 2021
Produced in Australia

ISBN 978 0 6487005 5 0 (print)
ISBN 978 0 6487055 6 7 (PDF e-book))

A catologuing-in-data entry for this book is available from the National Library of Australia: https://catalogue.nla.gov.au/

Contents

Dedications

For Beth Johnson

For her faith in me, her light and the beauty she left
imprinted in this World and in my heart.

For my three daughters

You are the beginning of this journey into my
'be-coming,' and you have always been and always
will be, my greatest teachers.

❧ 1 ❧

My Story

THE INSPIRATION behind writing this book was my own unique struggle with 'becoming' a mum. Every book I had picked up during pregnancy and afterwards would give me a general rundown on baby care, milestones, development, breastfeeding, and more overwhelming information such as **not** to co-sleep, education on sleep associations — and how **not** to create these so your new baby will sleep through the night. Ummm, whose new baby sleeps through the night, every night, without the boob? Ah, none of mine did!

I always felt like I needed to do more, be more, give more and almost always put the book down feeling more overwhelmed then when I picked it up.

Upon reflection and after having birthed three babies, reading a tonne of baby care books, and all the text books from my degree in maternal child and family nursing I decided that I wanted to read a book that was like a big warm hug, a book that was honest, that was mindful, open minded and little bit spiritual. One out of the pre-conceived box, one that delved into topics that I had to search far and wide for. A book that still gave me some beautiful gentle parenting tools that I could incorporate straight away. A book that hit me in my heart space and made me think about how I was raising my children. A book that asked the questions but not in textbook form.

So I started writing and this beautiful book evolved from there — from the depths of my being it wrote itself. There are vast amounts of knowledge, experience and evidence based research that I share in this book, but it is also based on ten years of mothering three very different daughters, with their births so unique, their journeys into becoming toddlers and little women, so extraordinary.

I will also share that for the first eight years of becoming a mama I was a registered nurse on an oncology ward, and during this time I gained a great sense of life, death, and purpose. The patients I looked after taught me a great deal about mindfulness, acceptance, surrender and trust. After I became a mum I realised that the values that were bestowed upon me in that period were actually lessons in life, a gift on my journey into parenting.

This book is a big piece of my heart. It's the letter that I wish I'd have been given when I birthed myself into motherhood. If only I'd known all or just some of the things within these pages, I know my first time experience into 'becoming' mum would have been felt with far more ease, grace and peace.

My journey into motherhood began 11 years ago, when I landed into motherhood hard. I say 'landed' loosely because it was more of a feeling of falling, and falling with a heavy-hearted thud.

My first birth was long: 25 hours of deep, deep waves, feeling engulfed and entrenched for most of it. I was induced at 42 weeks pregnant and laboured for the first 14 hours without anything other than a hand to hold and the back of the raised bed to grip and rip into with my throbbing body. After that 14 hours the midwife did a vaginal examination only to find that I was four centimetres dilated and our baby had turned into a posterior position which had my asshole swelling and me begging for an epidural. Unluckily, I reacted horribly to the fentanyl in the epidural and spiked a fever well over 40 degrees. I was convulsing and feverish.

Our baby had also spiked a temperature and was in foetal heart distress. I was closely monitored from that time onwards, under observation and very likely be prepped for an emergency caesarean. Hours went by and numerous obstetricians and midwives moved through the doors in my heated room.

Eventually, I was greeted by an obstetrician who explained that I would be put into stirrups so that he could check the baby's position and how far dilated I was. I remember looking at my husband's panicked face thinking "okay, I'm going to the theatre."

He did a vaginal examination and I was 10 centimetres dilated with our baby's head still three centimetres deep in my birth canal. He knew if I couldn't push her out we would lose her.

He was amazing. He had a dry sense of humour and a huge jar of *Vaseline*, along with the kindest face I'd placed eyes on in that time. He was what I desperately needed in that moment.

He told me about everything that he was doing as he was doing it. He was reassuring and continued to give me information in detail. I no longer felt out of control. He was the calm in my internal storm, a reassuring presence that Ben and I both needed.

I pushed our daughter as far down my birth canal as I could and from there he extracted her with a ventouse (a vacuum). Our daughter was born a translucent blue. Big dark eyes stared upon me. I knew she wasn't okay but I was so deliriously exhausted I could barely move my lips.

They took her straight to the emergency trolley and pumped out her tiny tummy, resuscitating her. Not long after that I was finally able to hold her on my chest, her heart beating upon mine. Skin to skin, the most beautiful creature I had ever placed eyes upon. I felt so unworthy of such a gift.

She stared at me then, right into my eyes she *seeked*. She knew. I knew. My heart lurched forward in my chest and in that pivotal moment I knew that I would never be the same again.

I was told that her oxygen was only at 80 percent, so she would be spending time in the special care nursery. I recall asking to breast-feed her, the midwife looked relieved that I had felt that way and helped her onto my breast. In time she pinked up and her oxygen saturations kept climbing then sat on the 100 percent mark.

She came into my room with me and hasn't left me since.

Throughout my hospital stay I had very little support during those long and noisy nights. We left two days later. My milk hadn't come in yet, but I couldn't stay a moment longer.

Our daughter cried from the very first day she landed Earth-side and didn't stop until four to five months later. There was certainly nothing peaceful about Ashta's arrival into my arms but it has been no less memorable since!

I remember vividly that for those nine months that I was pregnant the focus was solely on the pregnancy and birth, but no one told me what would happen after.

I knew that there would be a baby, but I was nowhere near prepared for her actual labour and I certainly was not in any way equipped for the ride that was Ashta. I was completely bombed from little to no sleep. She would sleep no longer than two hours both day and night.

After three months of Ashta being Earth-side we had tried almost everything to get even a small, three hour block of sleep — crying it out, leaving her in her cot for timed intervals then responding minutes later. I tried long walks and three am car trips, only to pull into the driveway an hour later and her eyes would spring open, and she would be wide awake.

Long and heated discussions with well-meaning family members, isolation, plus little contact with friends and family and a husband working two hours away, meant I was a time bomb of emotions and extreme sleep deprivation about to go off.

With time I became numb. I was the complete opposite of myself, unemotional and deliriously unhappy. I had two beautiful girlfriends with babies of the same age at that time, and they were amazing to have around, but at times I also felt much more guilt and sadness because I just couldn't "goo goo, gaa gaa" over my baby as they did.

What ran around my head instead was "what the fuck is wrong with her, and why won't she sleep?", "What the hell is wrong with me? Why don't I feel the same way that they do?'" I just couldn't understand that 'in love' feeling and I certainly didn't have it.

Around the 12 week mark post-partum we went to Tresillian where they 'trained' our baby to sleep, and during those six hours I felt like my soul was slowly being torn apart.

Don't get me wrong, I had attempted crying it out and at this point of sleep deprivation I was in no state to drive let alone look after an infant, **but** I had not expected it to be so brutal. Timed feeds, I was told not to wrap her the way that I wanted to, or that Ashta was used to, I had a counselling session where I cried the entire time and was 'diagnosed with post-partum depression,' only given a referral to see my general practitioner (GP) and no further guidance for my emotional state, afterwards.

No more than six hours later the midwife quietly slipped out of the room at Tresillian and said to me "I think your daughter has acute oesophageal reflux. I have changed her bedding several times today from her constant vomiting." My soul was shattered, my heart was broken and I literally cried the whole way home. I blamed the Doctor. How did he miss this? No wonder she can't sleep, she's so unwell. The guilt of what I had just put our then 12-week-old baby daughter through completely crushed me. Tresillian, I thought, was my **last** hope.

We did eventually get an official diagnosis by a new GP. He had a far more wholistic view on health — which we desperately needed. Ashta was put on *Zofran* and her sleep improved a little. By this stage her sleeping patterns had become something of a habit.

The overwhelming sadness of Ashta's birth and the first 12 weeks of her life felt much like an avalanche of emotions caving in on me, it truly shook me to the core in many ways.

Upon reflection, and when sleep finally came for us all, I realised how much my whole world had changed. I had lost friendships, and although we had parents nearby we had very little support due to their work hours. My husband was travelling two hours to and from work every day, and I felt completely numb and exhausted by it all.

I had a real and very sudden and overwhelming feeling of isolation; I felt alone and had an all-encompassing sadness grip my very being. I was crying all the time; tears would roll down my cheeks for no reason at all.

This feeling didn't go away until Ashta was at least 10 months old. By that time though my husband had lost his job and we were forced (due to not being able to pay the rent) to move into my parents' home. As my birthday rolled around that year, not long after moving into my childhood home, my husband forgot to buy me a card and I literally lost my legs, I collapsed into a crumbling mess.

It became obvious to my husband that something wasn't right. He finally recognised how I was feeling. Unfortunately, due to all of the changes in our life at the time he put it down to just that and went about seeking for work and study to provide for our family.

He found work at a surf shop but if we were to move out again it was up to me to continue in my nursing career. I had no other option but to return to work before I was ready. Prior to returning to work I saw a beautiful doctor who I worked with and who I trusted wholeheartedly. It was during this consultation that I was formally diagnosed with *post-partum depression.*

Post-partum depression is debilitating, isolating and it can often feel like someone has tuned off the lights as you literally muddle through it. There is no joy, you're only left with anxiety, sadness, and at times an intense feeling of inadequacy, and hopelessness. It is an illness that takes away the ability to access that joy at a time that you need it the most. Before that day I know now that I was literally in 'survival mode.'

This was the beginning of my breakdown. But ultimately the beginning of my *breakthrough* as a mother.

Rewinding back a little to Ashta's diagnosis, once we were educated on her illness and knew intuitively that it wasn't us or how we were parenting, we decided to finally listen to her needs. In doing so it inevitably led to us co-sleeping and continuing to breastfeed on demand without doubting ourselves anymore. At the time we didn't know there was a term for it, so we just followed what Ashta needed, what we needed. There were so many changes in her life that it made sense to us.

I had already been breastfeeding on demand, which I now view as the most amazing way to bond with your baby if you are able. I believe in many ways this connection kept me attached to her more than the other way around. Little did I know then that I needed that attachment and connection just as much as baby Ashta did.

Attachment parenting brought me back to an organic sense of motherhood, not a clinical orthodox one that I had fallen into. It allowed me to trust my own intuition and enabled me to connect and to consciously create my own 'twisting' path to motherhood, a journey that feels so good to my soul, brings joy into my life and now allows me to live within the present moments, even the tough and at times, overwhelming ones.

Completely unintentionally and without even knowing what that was, I started to trust myself as a mum and I began to listen to my intuition. We as parents decided to live consciously and make decisions based on what felt right for us. Our eldest daughter was, in fact, our greatest teacher.

Speaking with honest intention: we as parents can put an unrealistic expectation upon ourselves from the very beginning. As soon as our baby is within our arms we think that we need to know exactly what to do, when to do it and how. Where did this ridiculous idea come from?

The idea that we are supposed to know **everything** about how to care for our children before and after they are born? Intuitively, yes, but everything, no.

Parenting is not linear, it takes growth, it takes time, it takes nourishment and greater learning. Parenting is self-empowerment through gaining the knowledge that truly resonates with us.

This journey into my unique path into motherhood has led me here, to write this book. As a child and family nurse it is so easy to step into the role of practitioner and look at parenting as a set of tools to teach, educate and then tick off the list of 'to do's' in my clinic on any particular day.

But, as a mother, a woman and as a nurse, I want to consciously step far away from that form of practice. I want to educate, empower, support and inspire in a wholistic way. A realm that is rarely seen in clinics but it is needed now more than ever.

Parenting for me has been a balance between inner wisdom, conscious thought and action as well as reaching out for the science and the inner know-how.

I hope that my book can reach you in those places that need a little light shone upon it. It is a love letter for you, for all of the mamas who need a soft nudge to push you into your own intuitive knowing. My hope is that you will find inspiration that you will resonate with on this journey, and for those that need a warm hug or a never-ending hot cup of tea, these words were written for you.

2

The Fourth Trimester

"The more the child feels attached to the mother, the more secure he is in his acceptance of himself and the rest of the world. The more love he gets, the more he is capable of giving. Attachment is as central to the developing child as is eating and breathing."
Robert Shaw MD

YOU'VE GIVEN BIRTH You did it! Your incredible body and mind have just brought your little one Earth-side. There is a feeling of being overwhelmed that is honestly indescribable, but you are holding your beautiful, new baby within the warmth of your arms. You lift your baby up to nestle into their downy hair and smell their sweet newborn smell. In that moment that is all that matters, all that there is.

Those first exhausting, yet exhilarating days post-partum, will leave you breathless, exhausted, sore, but so very elated. Your days are filled with sweet smiles and never ending cries, moments that take your very breath away and at times moments that will leave you with a feeling of dread. You may feel overwhelmed by the relentlessness of it all, nappy changes, feeding for what can seem like hours, anxious about their sleep or lack of it. The days are long but the nights are longer. These are the days, the moments, the hours, when you embrace the opportunity to establish a solid foundation of trust. With this foundation the love grows, as does a healthy relationship between both you and your baby.

Welcome to the *fourth trimeste*r mama, embrace it wholeheartedly because it is **so** important.

I want to paint a picture for you, one that I hope will make clearer the very importance and value in this vulnerable time in your life as a new mama. I also would like to make it clear that no matter where you are on your parenting journey, all of your babies and you as a new mama deserve to feel valued, grounded and supported within this period after birth. Every time.

The fourth trimester begins once your little one is born. What I would like you to envision is your baby within your womb for nine months (maybe even ten months if you do pregnancy like me!) In this space and time **all** of your babies needs were wonderfully met. They didn't need to ask for food, sleep or have the uncomfortable feeling of a wet nappy, it was all undertaken from within.

Once Earth-side your little newborn now needs to cry when hungry, cry when tired, and cry when they are uncomfortable. This is the only way that babies know how to communicate. Your baby needs a gentle adjustment into their new world, and this is an essential time for bonding, nurturing and discovery. This is a significant learning period for both baby and you as you become fully mother. This is echoed in Associate Professor of Law, Saru M. Matambanadzo's article, *The Fourth Trimester*:

> *"The concept of a fourth trimester, drawn from maternal nursing and midwifery, refers to the crucial three to six month period after birth when many of the physical, psychological, emotional, and social effects of pregnancy continue. Giving this concept, legal relevance extends the scope of pregnancy beyond the narrow period defined by conception, gestation, and birth and acknowledges that pregnancy is a relational process, not an individual event."* [1]

I agree with this wholeheartedly. The fourth trimester is the period of time, whether three months, or six months, perhaps even a year, that you as a new mother are discovering, learning and creating a relationship with your new baby.

During your baby's time in the womb he is nourished, warm, jostled and rocked about. He wants for nothing. He feels safe and is bundled up tightly, always feeling cuddled. He hears your heartbeat, the sounds of your body digesting your food. He hears sounds and voices that surround you. He hears you and your partner's voice.

At birth your baby has developed enough in utero to experience life in this greatly less sheltered world. Within that moment of their birth there is already a fundamental change from being within a wet environment to then experiencing suddenly, a dry one. There is an abrupt change in temperature, and your baby needs to develop the ability to breath on his own; and yet another unexpected change from being in a head down position to suddenly experiencing a levelling up with the rest of his body. Newborn babies are remarkable; they can sustain these changes so quickly and so well, yet with few obvious symptoms.

In this huge new world, your baby is vulnerable. She is no longer in the womb but needs to be in your arms. She is happy, blissful and complete here; within your arms is where your connection with her will grow. This is where trust will flourish.

You may be feeling utterly exhausted in those first few days, because post-partum is exhausting. It's feeling sore, overwhelmed and perhaps even a little perplexed. It is completely okay and normal to feel like this, to feel so needed by this beautiful little human that you've created, carried and now birthed, you may ask yourself "how did I just do that?" Thoughts of, "okay, so now what do I do?" will most likely creep into your head and heart space, which is exactly why this period is so important to rest, nourish yourself and be nourished by those around you so that you can feed and tend to your baby's needs.

Fourth Trimester Treatments

There are many different ways in which eastern and western societies treat the fourth trimester. I want to explore a couple of these and hopefully help to create a sense of understanding around why the fourth trimester should be cherished and treated with far more presence and respect.

The post-partum period is better understood in native societies than in the more modern ones. It is usually within the first three to six weeks after birth that new mothers are pampered and taken care of. Post-partum practices for new mothers differ slightly according to where in the world and in what culture they are practiced, however, there are some overriding similarities.

Rest

Within most traditional cultures around the world new mothers are expected — and supported in their need — to rest deeply for at least the first 20 to 60 days following the birth of their new baby.

In India, it is said that the new mother should stay 'in, on or around the bed' for the first 40 days. Throughout this time, she is encouraged to be resting, sleeping or feeding her new baby. This period of rest will allow her body the time it needs to heal from the efforts of her pregnancy and birth and will significantly reduce her stress levels as she retreats from all household duties such as cleaning and cooking. Throughout this important period in a new mother's life, her baby is with her or being cared for by family members while she sleeps.

Warmth

In some cultures, new mothers are encouraged to keep warm. They consume warm, nourishing foods and are asked to avoid cold and/or raw foods. In other cultures, she is required to not wash her hair for the first few weeks post-partum.

In traditional Chinese medicine, an acupuncturist might also perform a 'mother roasting' where the new mothers abdomen is warmed with a Moxa stick before being bound up tightly.

Nourishment

In both the Chinese medicinal system and *Ayurveda* (traditional Indian medicine) a new mother's digestive system is known to be depleted immediately after her pregnancy and birth. Her digestive 'fire' (known as *Agni*) is known to have decreased which in turn leaves her susceptible to conditions such as indigestion, constipation, and gas as well as probably experiencing a huge drop in her energy.

Therefore, within the first 40 days it is important to feed the new mother with nutritious well cooked and easy to digest, warming foods. This will help increase and stimulate her digestive system as well as give her enough much needed energy to make nutritious, nourishing breast milk for her new baby.

Digestive spices such as ginger and turmeric will help to invigorate your digestion and help support you with elimination. Always try to choose foods that are warm, oily and also easy to digest. Soups, dahls, oatmeal, and rice puddings are ideal options. Try to not consume cold smoothies, raw salads and any foods that are not warming for your body.

Ingest fats that will feed your tissues and soothe your hormones and emotions. Ghee is a great choice, try to add it to all foods. (See also: https://www.roostbooks.com/ayurvedic-self-care-for-the-postpartum-parent/)

The list below provides a few ideas for warming Ayurvedic foods for your fourth trimester:

> **The sweet and sour of it** Foods that will taste of a sweet, sour or even salty flavour can help to rebuild tissue as well as promote rejuvenation.

> **Soupy and oily** The focus here is on consuming foods with these qualities to ensure easier digestibility for your stomach.

> **Always choose fresh** Foods that have been frozen in a packet from your local supermarket, or are canned, can be difficult for you to digest and does not promote optimal post-partum health.

Vegetarian food Meat holds a very heavy energy, and for this reason, it can be difficult on your sensitive digestive system. If you are not comfortable eating a complete vegetarian diet, than it will be important to incorporate some chicken and fish in your diet, bone broths and soups are amazing.

Spiced foods Some people believe that you will need to eat a bland diet in the days after your babies birth. Nothing could be further from the truth! You may choose to stay away from very hot chilies, onion and raw garlic, but most spiced seasonings will help to stimulate your digestive and some may even promote lactation!

Cooked well Food should always be warm and cooked thoroughly.

Iron-enriched foods Dark sugars such as molasses, maple syrup and even coconut sugars will give you much needed energy, these sweets can also build up your blood after giving birth. Dates, figs, and red grapes are good examples of iron-rich foods too.

You can read about similar foods here: https://shakticare.com/postpartum-diet-ultimate-guide/)

The fourth trimester is an important aspect of a woman's journey from being 'maiden' to 'mother'. As you can see, it is a common theme throughout so many parts of the world to celebrate and nourish the new mother. Doing so also gives a new mum the chance to be honoured for your important and incredible contribution, not only to your child but also to your community as a whole.

I feel that it is important to highlight that if you as a new mother are stressed, exhausted, hungry and feeling completely unsupported then stress hormones such as cortisol and adrenaline will also have an adverse effect on your oxytocin levels, this can potentially make the bonding process between you as a new mother and your baby more difficult to even begin, it can also affect the production of your breastmilk.

How to plan for your fourth trimester

Unfortunately for many of us, we do not have the means or support systems to enjoy a complete 40 days of rest. However, I sincerely believe that we can and should prioritise our post-partum in the same way we do our birth.

Here are a few tips you might like to consider so that you can have a beautiful fourth trimester.

Gather up your village It takes a well-meaning community to support you when you bring your new baby home.

If you have a handful of family and/or friends around, set up a meal train so that when they come to visit they do so with a meal to contribute for that night or which can be frozen for another time.

Don't be shy in asking for help, there is no shame in saying "would you mind hanging the laundry out, or putting a load of laundry on for me?"

Think outside the box if you don't have close family or friends around. Your *village* can be as varied as your midwife, a maternal child and family nurse, maybe your work colleagues, or you can pop some extra cash aside so that you can hire a cleaner occasionally. There are also so many pre-made meals available for home delivery now such as *Hello Fresh* and *Lite n' Easy* that could come in handy. Anything that will make your life easier and ensure you are well cared for.

Within this timeframe think of it as a 'staycation' in your own home, snuggled up with your new baby and being cared for by those around you. Think of all the things that bring you a sense of peace and joy, and do those things. Watch funny movies (laughing can increase your oxytocin and happy hormones), nap when your baby has a nap. I know this is a totally cliché but your future self will thank you, I promise!

Most importantly, surround yourself with all of the beautiful things that make your heart happy: good books and magazines, a never-ending cup of warm tea, crystals, books to feed your soul, and don't forget to call on your people when necessary.

There will be many opportunities to take your new baby out into the world or receive truckloads of visitors, but be sure to first make those first few weeks a time just for the two of you and those closest.

Your fourth trimester doesn't have to be a time of exhaustion, stress and overwhelm, but instead it can be a time that's honoured and valued, a time of deep transformation, the 'becoming' of mother. This is for you, and for your new baby.

Ina May Gaskin, author of *Spiritual Midwifery*, explains it this way:

> *"In Western society most women go home expecting to go home and cope with new motherhood virtually alone during the postpartum weeks. Most women are dealing with postpartum pain and discomfort, healing episiotomies, sore full breasts and the exhaustion of broken sleep. Is it any wonder that postnatal depression is one of the most common post birth complications in Western society?"* [2]

Hormones and feelings

Let's look at another important aspect of the fourth trimester. Hormones and emotional well-being can tend to be overlooked but I am very aware of this aspect of care being missed, not only due to my own experience of post-natal depression but also due to the misunderstanding surrounding it.

Many women will tend to be weepy when their milk comes in. This is known as the three-day baby blues. It is a mild change in your mood as a new mum and it may be characterised by irritability, tearfulness, anger, tension and perhaps some mild anxiety.

As mothers there is a fake ploy that says we 'should' feel happy, elated and madly in love with our new baby. Perhaps this is due to societal pressure and our own increased expectations on what motherhood should 'feel' like, for me, I didn't fall in love with our daughter until she was at least four weeks old. I felt overwhelmed, bone tired, emotional. She cried all the time and so did I. There were many moments when I thought 'is this all there is?'

I want you to know that these feelings and emotions are an unexpected surprise, but they are normal. After all, your whole world has been turned upside down.

These are feelings that I had — and you may have too — and they can be somewhat disturbing and even isolating, especially if you as a new mum has any 'ill' feelings towards your baby or you may even feel like your new baby is 'ordering you around' or 'refusing to sleep or feed.' Yes, these feelings are disturbing, but they are there and also far more common than most realise.

Fourth trimester changes

Now, let's look at your fourth trimester and all the changes that are happening, physically, mentally and spiritually.

Exhaustion

Your body has just completed **the** most physically and mentally exhausting event of your entire life. A long trail of hormones will flood every pore of your being. You are learning about each other on the 'outside,' and it can be incredibly overwhelming.

Relentless hours of breastfeeding, hours of nappy changes, holding and nursing your baby in the wee hours of the morning, settling them off to sleep only to have to resettle them minutes later; there are so many changes in our lives at this stage it can feel like the merry go round will never end.

The baby blues

It is very common to feel weepy and moody shortly after giving birth. Having a baby can be both exhilarating and exhausting. It can bring much joy, but it can also challenge you in ways you never expected.

You may feel exhausted, worried, unhappy, or trapped, and find yourself crying over things that usually would not bother you. Your appetite might increase or decrease, and you may find yourself unable to sleep. You might be irritable, nervous, anxious and feeling worried about being a 'good' mum, or afraid that motherhood will never feel good, or be right for you.

I want you to know that these feelings are absolutely normal during the first couple of weeks after giving birth, in fact, 'up to 80 percent of new mum's experience these 'baby blues' according to statistics from the Royal Women's Hospital in Melbourne. [3]

What causes the baby blues?

The baby blues can be triggered by the physical changes that happen after birth, or emotional factors, or both. Your body changes rapidly, your hormone levels begin to drop, your breasts become engorged as your milk starts to come in, and you will most likely be bone-tired and exhausted.

These very real and overwhelming changes can be enough to bring on the baby blues. Emotionally, you may feel incredibly anxious about your baby's wellbeing, you might feel that the transition to motherhood, or adjusting to your new routine is too much. Your very new responsibilities as a mum can leave you feeling discouraged.

What can you do to feel better?

The baby blues will tend to go away with time, usually within the first two to three weeks. Even though you're adjusting to the daunting and very real reality of having to meet a tiny human's every need, it's important not to neglect yourself in the process. This is easier said than done, of course, but don't be shy in, again, asking for help.

Throughout the first few weeks post-partum the very best thing that you can do to nourish yourself so that you can concentrate on the very real task of nourishing your new baby is to rest when baby does, as clichéd as that sounds, sleep deprivation can make the baby blues feel so much worse, try to make an effort to rest whenever you can.

Rest can look like reading a magazine or a book, laying out on your sunny lawn, even a 10-minute nap can help. And, as I mentioned previously, be sure to ask for support from friends and family.

These suggestions can make a huge difference in helping you to feel better and more able as a new mum.

Grounding yourself daily is a non-negotiable principle, getting out, breathing in the fresh air, feeling your naked feet in the grass or on the sand can help to earth you. Being grounded can mean two things:

- Being fully present in your body and/or
- Feeling connected to the earth.

We've all experienced being grounded. We feel 'at home' in ourselves and in our bodies, it's an essential aspect of creating a better well-being for both body and mind.

After a few days try to get in some light exercise daily — a slow but grounded walk in the fresh air can do wonders for your mood. (If you had a c-section or still feel sore from your delivery, you may want to check with your healthcare provider first.)

Your mental health as a new mama is an important aspect of creating room to move out of the confines of the baby blues, and to lean into the people who care about you. If you have a partner, share how you've been feeling and what you might find helpful.

Maybe you have a trusted friend or family member who can also offer a listening ear, even some hands-on help with your baby or the housework once your partner is back at work.

How can I tell if I have post-partum depression?

It is easy to confuse the baby blues with post-partum depression because they have some symptoms in common. What I will say is that while the baby blues tends to ease with time, post-partum depression does not. It also tends to be far more intense, so if you are feeling sad, lonely, depressed, symptoms of anxiety such as heart palpations persist, you need to seek help from a trusted GP who can look into possible treatment options.

During those first few weeks in your post-partum you may experience fluctuating feelings of anger, anxiety, guilt, hopelessness, loss of interest or pleasure in activities, mood swings, or even panic attacks

Be aware that crying, irritability, and restlessness as well as whole body fatigue and loss of appetite can be changes within ourselves which can be difficult to bear — but they are absolutely normal.

As a new mother you may also experience cognitive changes such as a lack of concentration or even unwanted thoughts. You may feel depressed or even fearful for your future, "will this be my everyday from now on?" Also common may be insomnia or repeatedly going over and over your thoughts

The American Mayo Clinic has more information about post-partum symptoms here: https://www.mayoclinic.org/diseases-conditions/postpartum-depression/symptoms-causes/syc-20376617?

So how do you know which one you have?

If you're in the first couple of weeks post-partum, be sure to expect some emotional as well as physical upheaval. There are so many changes developing and evolving it is completely normal to feel somewhat lost and overwhelmed, teary and fearful throughout those initial weeks. But if you continue to feel this way for longer than three weeks after giving birth, be sure to seek help and call a trusted practitioner.

Take care of your space as a new mum, keep visitors to a minimum, only allow those that don't take your energy, the givers in your life to have the opportunity to visit. This space in your fourth trimester is sacred, it's a time that you are all learning about one another, taking baby steps into becoming a family. There is plenty of time for those around you to meet your new baby.

Please be sure to also give yourself permission to take care of you. Insist that you rest as much as possible, as well as eating nourishing warm foods, create a schedule and set priorities of the things that must be done versus the things that can wait, like doing the laundry or making dinner. Again, be sure to ask visitors to bring along a nourishing dish that can be frozen for this particular laying-in time.

Be your own advocate for what you need at a crucial time in your life when you are 'becoming' a mother, whether you are already a mum or if you haven't been a mum before, there is no instruction manual or guidebook for you, post birth. Each birth is unique as is each baby, so give yourself the much needed space and time to create the necessary foundations to start your new life as a mama in a wholistic, calm and nurturing way.

The sacred fourth trimester

Birth is a coming of rites passage, it is an event marking an important stage in your life. You are maiden coming into motherhood. It is a sense of innate self-empowerment, an inner strength you did not even realise you had, the kind of strength that is primal, deep and raw.

Birth is healing, and it is a new beginning. Those days after your new baby has arrived are the most intense. The long days are magical. It is mama milk being miraculously produced by your own body. It is being up all night waiting for the trickles of sunlight to ride in on a new day. It is love soaked days and newborn smells every damn day.

Despite feeling sore, having an achy back, with itchy, stretched skin, it is even happening amongst the cold pots of coffee and feeling like there's never enough time in your day. You will find yourself steal-ing those moments of fleeting time sitting, laying, holding and just 'being' with your little one.

You will find yourself caught off-guard by the unexpected, almost painful intensity and depths of love and attachment, protectiveness, and care that you have never felt before and don't quite know what to do with. This love is the love only a mother can feel in the deepest depths of her soul. It is the kind of love that is entrenched in our very bones, the love of your newborn baby.

The fourth trimester is a time for connection. You are both learn-ing about each other on the outside. It can be an overwhelming time as you both stumble through the new knowledge that comes with a new breastfeeding journey, whether this is your first, second, or third baby. It is always a new journey because each baby is uniquely them, therefore it will take time, patience and a healthy dose of accepting what is happening on your breastfeeding journey, or possibly, what is *not* happening.

This period of vulnerability will flow on into how you feel before you were 'mum.' Amongst the dripping nipples, endless nappies and clothes that no longer fit, you will feel like you are not you anymore.

Your fourth trimester is a time for trust. Trusting and leaning into your own feelings, those feelings within the depths of your stomach that tell you if it feels okay or maybe that it doesn't, this feeling is the very essence of a new space for intuition, something that only you uniquely have as a mother to your baby.

You have gone from a state or 'being' to 'becoming.' Your body might not feel like it's yours anymore because it is completely different (again). It is different to the body you had before you were pregnant. Different to your body blooming with baby. Different again now that you have brought your baby Earth-side. You may be breastfeeding around the clock, you may not even feel your core anymore (but it's there!) you are sore, bruised, swollen and may even have a few stitches. This, my friend, is all completely normal. Welcome to your unique fourth trimester, a time for stillness, a greater learning and nourishment for self and your newborn baby.

There is a lot to ponder over within these first few weeks with your baby. Your ever-evolving body has just brought forth a human being. Your body has grown a small human. Your body has facilitated your little one's growth and development such as budding a placenta, umbilical cord and creating the space for your body to accumulate fluid to cushion your baby. It has also pushed every organ that was already taking up rent to numerous other spaces to accommodate your little human and its helpers.

So of course, your body will have changed again once your baby is born. Right now, you may be feeling like it will never be the same again. It will. With time and a bucket full of patience. With a lot of love for self and nurturing of you and all that you have achieved. Some pieces of you will heal quicker than others and that's okay. It has taken you nine glorious months to evolve into 'mother' and it will take a little longer again to gain your footings not only in body but in mind too.

You are only just beginning, and it is a transformative time. A time to *become*. A time to accept what is and what has just begun. A time to lean in together as parents but also you as a new mum getting to know your new baby. This time is about growth, healing, and evolving into the conscious and intuitive family that you have previously envisioned.

This period beyond and following your new baby's birth will be the most remarkable part of life outside of your womb. What your baby will encounter within these first moments is how she will **feel** that the nature of her life will inevitably **be**.

This is the time that you are also 'becoming,' mother. Remember that each baby is an individual with its own unique set of needs and wants. You, as a mother, have maternal instincts that are built within you, so when you are able to open up your heart space, and in turn learn to trust yourself and all that your body achieved in nourishing and comforting your baby, you will realise that you are already connected with what your baby needs, you already know the way.

&3&

Introduction to Attachment Parenting

ATTACHMENT parenting is one of those terms where parents either cringe or show a strong interest in learning more. For myself and my husband we kind of just 'fell' into an attachment parenting kind of life.

Don't get me wrong, we had always envisioned parenting to be about creating a deep relationship with our children, one that was built upon trust and that no doubt would start with connection and attachment; because breastfeeding your baby and cuddling them is attachment parenting yes?

What we learned, though, as new parents was that attachment parenting is more about an **intuitive** approach to parenting. It is about listening to your baby's cues and allowing them to tell you what it is that **they** need. When we started doing that rather than me trying to 'control' the situation whether that was controlling sleep or timing feeds because my breasts were so sore and engorged, or at times thinking to myself "ah I'm so spent I honestly can't pick you up anymore!" When I finally started to trust in my baby my own approach to parenting shifted.

Our attachment journey started with me *baby-wearing*, our baby had severe oesophageal reflux so she liked to be held and upright, baby-wearing took the pressure off me needing to 'always pick her up,' because she was already there and happy too. As a new mama I went with my babies breastfeeding needs which weren't timed, so breastfeeding on demand was commonplace for us and was our experience for as long as our baby wanted.

I started to develop an intuitive parenting muscle that I didn't even know existed by listening to our new baby's needs, which meant I wasn't fighting for control and finally welcoming in the ebbs and flows more. Days were still long, as were the nights, but I felt like I was okay, and that our baby was okay, too.

As mothers our bodies alone are an amazing source of strength, we develop an incredible flood of natural hormones which help us to create attachment and connection during, and post birth. These are designed to help us mother as well as more easily attune to our new baby's needs by learning to flex our intuitive parenting muscles. This is the beginning of an *Attachment Parenting* relationship.

As Susan Krauss Whitbourne says in her article in *Psychology Today*, 'The 4 Principles of Attachment Parenting and Why They Work. A sensible guide to make attachment parenting work for you':

"Attachment theory emphasizes the nature of the relationship between children and their caregivers (usually their parents). It has it's roots in observations made by psychiatrists in World War II who noted the impaired physical, psychological, and social development of infants in hospitals and orphanages who were separated from their parents. After recognizing that these children needed not just food but

physical contact, the caregivers noticed vast improvements in their development." [4]

When we can respond to our baby's cries; breastfeed on 'demand' for an extended period; 'wear' our babies in a carrier or a sling; as well as use gentle ways to help our baby get off to sleep, we can develop wholistic ways to approach an 'attachment parenting' aspect to our parenting journey.

To be clear, you do not need to incorporate **all** of these app- roaches. It is about being open to your baby's needs and listening to what it is that they want. A quick and relatable example — our eldest daughter loved all of the cuddles, so she loved to co-sleep, but our middle daughter wasn't a super cuddly baby and instead she loved her space when she slept (she still does!) so co-sleeping, as much as we loved it, wasn't going to work for her.

Our story as parents started 11 years ago when we 'accidentally' started co-sleeping with our first baby due to her oesophageal reflux.

After experiencing many different realms of sleep training due to our baby only sleeping for two to three stints at any one time, it was only when we 'tripped' into attachment parenting and safe co- sleeping that life with our then three-month-old baby changed for the better. I finally felt like the mother that I wanted to be, which I knew intuitively felt right for me.

It was that kind of sleep deprivation and post-natal depletion, and eventually the actual 'breakdown' that brought me to my 'breakthrough' and to a topic that is now very close to my heart: *safe co-sleeping*, a subject at times opposed by Western society.

As Jan Hunt author of *The Natural Child, Parenting from the Heart,* says: "We are moving toward an artificial, mistrustful, and dis- tant approach, especially in the Western world." [5]

When a mother sleeps next to or near her baby (I would suggest a side cart bassinet that you can attach to your bed), she is more able to use the instinctive responses that a new mother has, such as those similar to hearing her new baby's first cry. This also prevents the need for hard crying that can be so stressful to the baby and the entire family.

Renowned American Paediatrician Dr William Sears has said:

"Often times I felt ridiculous giving my seal of approval to what was in reality such a natural thing to do, sort of like reinventing the wheel and extolling its viruses. Had parent's intuition sunk so low that some strange man had to tell modern women that it was ok to sleep with their babies?"

When babies sleep near their parents, you are able to create a sense of trust and security for them, acceptance of them being in your life, and unquestionably you are showing them that your love is without condition.

Co-sleeping with your baby safely, for example in a 'co-sleeper' (you can buy these online or as an attachment to your own bed) and minimising the separation from your baby during the first few months is an absolute lifesaver. In fact, 50 to 80 percent of parents bed-share in countries like Australia, the US and the UK. However, I would very much like to emphasise the 'safe' side of safe co-sleeping, because it is quite different to having a baby 'share' a room with you!

Safe co-sleeping

"With increased maternal contact and feeding, crying is significantly reduced, and contrary to conventional thinking, maternal and infant sleep can be increased." James J Mckenna PhD

Putting our new baby into their crib in another room, isolated and alone, felt completely wrong to us, for us a bassinet in our room and bed sharing with a co-sleeper made for much easier breastfeeding during the night and much more sleep.

Being with our daughter all the time and always closely connected allowed us to really get to know her needs. With an increased knowledge base, life with our new baby evolved into being an easier journey and we felt far more confident in the decisions that we were making.

> *"Attachment to your infant is where your infant will use you as their primary caregiver as a secure base from which they can then explore and when necessary use you as a haven of safety as well as a great source of comfort."* [6]

Attachment parenting is not a set of 'rules,' it is about creating secure attachments in simple ways such as responding to your infant's distress in sensitive and 'loving' ways, such as picking them up when they are upset and reassuring them that you are all there for them.

Your baby will feel nothing short of secure in the knowledge that you are present and connected. They will feel that they can freely express their negative emotions knowing that it will only elicit comfort and love from you.

Communication with your baby begins at birth

Time and time again with our first newborn baby, I was told I was "spoiling her by holding her too much", "just let her cry", "you'll spoil her by feeding on-demand."

I have since learned that 'spoiling' is one of those mindless ideas that get passed down from generation to generation, even though on the surface it is absolutely ludicrous!

Dr Bob Jacobs, author of *Perfect Parents, Perfect Children: Changing the World by Celebrating our Perfection,*[7] says: "a newborn baby only asks for what he or she needs. In every species, it is the role of the parent (usually the mother) to provide what the baby needs. It is only in our species that we question the natural wisdom inherent in this behavior." When you as a new mum respond to your baby's cries you will only teach them good things, that they are loved, that they are important, and that they can trust you.

Attunement or as I like to call it, **intuitive** parenting is exactly that, listening to you, the parent. How does it make you feel when your baby is crying? Is your innate urge to pick her up? Then do that. Do you feel like your beautiful infant might need some milk? Then do that too.

Too often we allow other people's well-intentioned advice to flow through our brains and imprint its way onto our hearts. Too often we are *Googling* "crying baby" on our smartphones only to forget that we already know the answer. We already have that intuitive wisdom inbuilt within us; it is in our heads, our hearts, our wombs.

There is no doubt that a baby's cry creates stress, as Jean Liedloff says in *The Continuum Concept*: "A baby's cry is precisely as serious as it sounds."[8] An infant crying should not be a power struggle. It should be thought of as an opportunity to connect. It is healthy communication. All babies need to have the opportunity to grow with a generous capacity for love, connection, and trust.

Let's be honest here, no-one likes to have their communication ignored. Think carefully and be honest: how would you feel if you were so upset, stamping your feet, crying, screaming and your partner just left you there, just like that? You would feel angry, hurt, vulnerable and abandoned. This will inevitably damage your relationship, will it not? So why do we adults feel that it is okay to do that to our own babies?

Peace starts from birth, yes, but it is also within the four walls of our home that peace is truly created. We generate imprints within our children in this period. Being a parent creates the opportunity to begin reparenting ourselves when we can make sense of our own early experiences, this is when we are able to create what we want with our own children.

I'll use my own early experiences as an example: I was deemed an emergency caesarean, but I knew that I didn't want a caesarean (even though it very nearly did happen) and I wanted to breastfeed even though I was a bottle fed baby. We have choices. We get to choose how we would like to raise our children, from the very beginning, it all begins at birth.

Newborns are born *connecting*. It is important to understand that a loving responsive interaction is essential for that beautiful connection and building trust with your newborn baby. Touch is as important and fundamental as food, therefore gentle beginnings are essential for your confidence as a new mama and for the trust to develop between you and your infant.

As Jean Liedloff points out:

"We have had exquisitely precise instincts, expert in every detail of child care, since long before we became Homo sapiens. But we have conspired to baffle this long-standing knowledge so utterly that we now read a million books on how we should behave and raise our own children."

Full disclosure ... I have done this. I second-guessed my instincts and my intrinsic knowledge of what my baby's needs were. However, as new parents, we decided to take back our power and read only what resonated with us (which I hope is this book you're reading right now!) rather then what was recommended by the professionals around us.

We chose to dive head first into *trust*, trusting that our baby knew what they needed, whether that was to be fed, comforted, a nappy change or a sleep, we needed to believe in our own instincts as well, that it was okay to not be in a 'routine' at 12 weeks old, to know innately that sleep training wasn't what we needed or even wanted. We needed to begin thinking consciously, discussing our infant's care, and making decisions together, trusting and using our instinctual knowledge.

I am not going to go so far as to say it was easy, but finally, being the parents that were working together as a team and making decisions based on what felt right, began to feel natural for us. The experience of being able to comfort our child intuitively cracked open our hearts and we fell more and more in love with her and with being parents.

Night-time parenting

Parenting your baby at night-time is not about a set of rules and sleep strategies. Parenting your baby at night-time is about **connection**.

As a new parent I was shocked to find myself feeding my new baby literally around the clock. Eight weeks into being a new mama I was desperate for sleep! As I mentioned earlier, we tried *everything* but it just didn't feel right.

Fortunately for myself and my husband we didn't continue the 'sleep training' merry-go-round, we found ourselves co-sleeping and I continued to breastfeed our little love to sleep.

Yes, as new parents there is no doubt that you will find yourselves shocked to the core in the realisation that your new baby feeds around the clock. But did you know that the average new baby will sleep for up to 19 hours of a 24-hour day, but some may sleep for as little as eight.

All babies are **unique**.

In those first few weeks post-partum your new baby will wake, feed and then fall asleep again. Only to wake no more then two to three hours later, yes, for yet another feed. As your new baby grows so does their appetite, you will find your baby will want bigger feeds as opposed to more frequent feeds, they will tend to be more active between feeds also, which will then (fingers crossed) allow hopefully, for a deeper and longer sleep later in the day.

If you can find yourself listening more to what your baby needs and if you can grow in bravery and lean into that, you will find yourself softening rather than becoming increasingly more rigid within your 'sleep' approach.

What your baby needs is a loving, responsive interaction with you, always. This is an essential foundation for connection and the beginning of building trust. Your touch is just as important and as fundamental as the food that you provide for them.

There is absolutely **no** doubt that infancy is challenging, but babies are simply too young and inexperienced to handle their own causes for crying — whatever that may be — sleep, a change of nappy, needing to be fed again but more so for comfort, or just because they feel overwhelmed and they need you.

It is up to you as their parent, to take responsibility in meeting your baby's needs, their need for nurturing from you, your security and unconditional love. And if I am being honest, we as parents, as human beings need that too. As humans we long for connection and affection. So why shouldn't our little one's needs be met for this too?

Let's move back to that omnipresent terminology, 'sleep ass-ociations.' Who has been told **not** to breastfeed their little one to sleep??

Most babies will need milk during the night within their first year. Many milestones are slowly developing and then happening; for example, crawling, first words, and walking. Their brains are develop-ing at lightning speed, there are mental leaps, teeth erupting, illness. The list goes on.

They will always get back into their own rhythm once they are past whatever it is that is going on for them. In the meantime give them what they need, which is you, and no doubt your comforting breastmilk.

Breastfeeding creates that beautiful and much needed loving connection for you both. When you are breastfeeding your little love to sleep at night your milk has already developed the amazing hormones that are specific for that settling feed.

Melatonin is one of the peaceful, sleep inducing hormones that is released, and then there is oxytocin, a wonderful 'feel good, relaxation' hormone that is released for the both of you. Your breastmilk creates a wonderful concoction of hormones to help your little love get off to sleep. So why wouldn't you use it!?

Another sleep association I am going to dive into is 'spoiling.' This is yet another well-used term within Western society and is all about nursing and holding your baby too much.

It is instinctive to rock your beautiful new baby and to hold them, and it has been done for millennia. Think of your fourth trimester with your new baby as an extension of your pregnancy because for nine (or ten months if you do pregnancy like me!) long months they have been with you, listening to your heartbeat from the inside.

Why wouldn't they still want and need that beautiful comfort? Who 'decided' that breastfeeding, rocking, and cuddling your new baby off to sleep was taboo and creating 'sleep associations' or the other good one that I love, 'creating a rod for your back!' Whatever happened to creating healthy attachment?

Co-sleeping — yet another controversial subject

I know that desperation of no sleep first-hand, as explained earlier, after a long and traumatic delivery of our first daughter. Once home, we discovered she would sleep no longer than two hours at a time, day or night. Unfortunately for her, she was misdiagnosed early on and her sleeplessness was due to a severe case of oesophageal reflux.

Prior to that diagnosis and due to our desperation, we had tried everything. Crying it out, leaving her in her cot for timed intervals responding minutes later. We tried long walks and car trips, but she would still end up wide awake.

There were long and heated discussions with well-meaning family members, very little contact with friends and wider family and a husband working two hours away. I was a time bomb of emotions about to go off. It was at that point I realised that getting up every two hours, rocking our baby to sleep and breastfeeding for an hour, every night was getting to be too much for myself and my family.

Safe co-sleeping saved my sanity, it saved my marriage and it created a connection that I so desperately needed. Put simply, when you as a mother sleep next to your baby you are more able to use your own instinctive responses that every new mother has, it is a very similar instinct to your reaction to your baby's first cry.

Practical tip: if you are worried about placing your infant between yourself and your partner you can always use a snuggle bed to put between you both or move the basinet to be right next to you and the bed. Whenever in doubt simply ask yourself: **is it safe?** Is it respectful? And does it feel right intuitively for you and your family? If you answered *yes* to any of these questions, then do what feels right for you because that is what your baby needs.

And if there is only one thing that you take away from reading this, I want you to remember: **Sleep is only a problem if it is a problem for you and your family.**

Attachment Parenting

Attachment parenting and co-sleeping can no doubt be demanding due to all of the 'holding,' therefore, It is really important to understand that **your** wellbeing as a parent is also **so** essential to your baby's emotional adjustment, their secure attachment. You need to make time for you too, a cuppa with a good book out in the sunshine, a walk on the beach with your little one bundled up in a carrier.

Make sure to earth yourself daily. You can do this simply by taking your shoes off and purposefully go out into your front or backyard and feel the grass between your toes, get outside into the garden. Whatever it is that you can do to get much needed grounding will be wonderful for your mental health.

Attachment parenting can be defined as simply leading with love, but also when we have love for ourselves too, than we will always have room to lead with love and attachment for our babies. We will also exceed **all** of our baby's simple needs and expectations from the very start.

As it was, it still took us a good few months with our first daughter to realise that all we really had to do was to follow her lead, and to trust our own instincts as parents, when we did do that, parenting for us became less stressful, our expectations dropped completely, and we felt far more confident in our very new role, a raw and heart expanding journey called 'parenting.'

Peace begins at birth, yes, but I do strongly believe that it starts more so within the initial post-partum period. This is your baby's expected place within your arms. If your baby is always brought to your chest in upset as well as in happy times, they will know attachment, they will know security and safety, and they will always know love.

❧ 4 ❧

Bonding with your baby

INFANCY CAN BE, and is, challenging. We will all experience it differently and it is not up to us to compare, yet I do feel that we need to begin to share — share our unique stories in order to honour them and others experience of 'becoming mum.'

'Becoming mum,' can have you feeling overwhelmed and not necessarily bonding straight away with your new baby. Despite what the social media and magazine images look like, its not always like that for every mother initially.

When our first-born daughter was finally Earth-side, I didn't 'feel' a lot of anything. I was numb from the epidural and the 26-hour labour. I was numb with the trauma of watching my newborn baby resuscitated and having her stomach pumped out. I was numb with the thought of what to do now? I was numb to the intensity of it all. It took me many, many weeks to 'feel' anything toward her ... to finally feel something of a connection.

My experience of post-partum depression wasn't swift. It was a slow burn. I felt like it was a slow and steady undoing of who I thought I was, into who I was becoming, a mother. I was scared to death of who that mother was or was going to be. I remember looking at our daughter and thinking to myself as she was happily playing, 'I really don't know what I'm doing, I don't know what to do with you.'

Upon reflection, I was always maternal, I looked after my little brother and sister a lot as we grew up and I especially thought of my little brother like a 'baby' to me, but it's very different when you're a mother yourself, when you can't just 'give them back,' — they're yours to love, nurture and take care of. I really didn't know how to do that, I felt completely incompetent and to be frank, I hadn't been around many babies before. I was the first of my friends to fall pregnant and so their understanding was minimal as well.

My family were nearby but worked full time, and I later learned that their expectation of me was that I would 'ask' for help if I needed it because they didn't want to 'intrude.' The last thing that I had the emotional capacity to do was to 'ask for help,' I didn't even know how to start my day, every damn day.

There were many, many factors that contributed to my spiral into post-partum depression. I literally felt like my world was spinning around and falling apart as I knew it. I had no idea about the ins and outs of taking care of a baby, let alone taking care of myself.

I didn't know how to ask for 'help.' I honestly thought my friends and family would just 'offer' up their support. I cried so much most days. I could not stand to be home because she would scream and vomit all day long. I was a flood of hormones. I felt like I was literally fighting for her and my survival daily. I did eventually ask for help and it came in the form of a local doctor with whom I worked.

Due to being forced to work again before I was ready after our daughter was ten months old. I saw one of my favourite doctors, someone I worked with at the time. He diagnosed me with post-partum depression but he clearly said that with all I had experienced so far and the intense lack of support and sleep he would not medicate me. Instead, he suggested a daily dose of *St John's Wort* so that I had the emotional and mental capacity to work through my emotions and bond with my baby.

I have since acquired maternal child and family nursing qualification, but at the time I was an oncology nurse and I had nothing to do with babies. However, I knew instinctively that babies were simply too young, and developmentally unable to self soothe, and that they shouldn't have to — *and* we shouldn't have to go through the trauma of it. They need us, and we need them.

Once I started to share my story I quickly realised that I was not alone. Many parents had babies who had oesophageal reflux. Many parents had experienced not 'feeling' connected or bonded to their baby straight away. Many parents had felt their highest highs and their lowest low. Many had attempted 'sleep training' and were now co-sleeping like myself. One of my hugest discoveries was that once we start to open up, piece by piece, we crack open our story and quickly learn that we are not alone.

This brings me back to the post-partum period, or otherwise and beautifully known as the fourth trimester. The fourth trimester is a time of intimacy, connection and nurture, both for mum and their new baby.

Our babies have been rocked constantly in utero. They have never had to ask for anything, not for food, and certainly not for sleep it is all given to them with great love from the vessel that they are growing in, our bodies, So why once they are Earth-side do we as a society question the importance of this crucial stage in our lives? Why do we question parents who wish to go to their baby when they are crying and why do we feel that new babies are developmentally able to self-soothe?

We bring our newborns home and decide to create walls, literal walls such as having them sleep in their own room within a cot, alone. I realise that co-sleeping is foreign to some or perhaps even taboo but co-sleeping in a bassinet or co-sleeper in your room is so **important**. It is the most effective way to sense their needs such as feeding, comfort and even SIDS (Sudden Infant Death Syndrome).

According to a recent article on the British *Red Nose* website about sharing a sleep surface:

> *"Red Nose recommends sleeping a baby in a cot next to the parents' bed for the first six to twelve months of life as this has been shown to lower the risk of SUDI."* [9] (Sudden Unexpected Death in Infancy)

Prams are often seen as a necessity, but when they have known nothing but the warmth within why not show your baby that *their* needs matter too. Your new baby's needs are very simple, and need not be overcomplicated, all that they seek is nurturing, security and love.

Wearing your baby in a carrier or sling can be the most beautiful way to create comfort for your infant with the soothing beat of your heart. It is a perfect way for your partner to also bond with them.

After my experience with our first daughter and then the unique, healthy births that followed with our next two, I quickly realised that the connection I missed with our first daughter in the ways of attachment may have contributed to the lack of feelings I initially felt for her (other than the trauma of her birth).

The bonding that I missed right after her birth made it difficult for me to establish breastfeeding. Unfortunately, 11 years ago we had no idea about how to educate ourselves on anything that would take place once we brought our new baby home, all that was given was about the birth itself.

Now, with my more in-depth education and experience as a maternal child and family nurse, I know that birth can be completely out of your control no matter how deeply you've delved into it. Post-partum though, you do have control over it, you can have a say in how you'd like it to be. You can choose the thread in which you'd like to weave your new parenting journey.

With the knowledge I have gained both personally as well as within my professional experience, I have acquired a deep passion and respect for the fourth trimester so I wanted to share with you a few tips to help strengthen and deepen those foundational bonds between you and your infant in the initial hours after your birth.

The first few hours

Connection is key

Eye contact with your new baby, is so simple yet so poignant. Imagine for a moment that you are in a strange new world, abducted by two strangers with a strange language, and you are entirely dependent upon them for all of your needs, hunger, thirst and comfort. This is a scary scenario and one that you could easily imagine for your new baby.

By giving your new baby a smooth and loving transition from womb to Earth-side, your baby will quickly realise that distress will lead to comfort. That their new world outside of the safety net of your womb is both warm and comfortable, it is still a place of nurture and safety within your arms. Don't expect to 'feel' anything, just 'be' there in that moment, just you and them.

Skin to Skin Contact

This is an essential key to emotional development for you both. Also, allowing this time and space for skin-to-skin contact will help to release a swell of oxytocin facilitating the hormonal work of bonding with your new baby. The first snuggle is not just 'good' psychology, it is the best overall type of 'medicine.' Newborns easily become cold so skin-to-skin contact creates a natural warmth, your baby also gets to know your heartbeat on the 'outside' that sense of familiarity is always comforting.

Encourage your little one to nestle into your chest. Once he or she starts to suckle at your breast they will calm down and start to feel more and more secure within your arms. Suckling at your breast also stimulates that elusive and magical hormone oxytocin which will, in turn, help to stimulate your uterus to contract, thus also minimising the possibility of a post-partum bleed.

Time

Give you and your new baby time. Time to get to know each other on the 'outside.' it's absolutely okay for you to not feel 'okay' and in love straight away. Time will facilitate that feeling and intense bond as you get to know each other on your new journey as **mum**.

It's important to request privacy once you've both been given the all-clear, whether you're still in hospital or at home. This will enable an intimacy to begin between the three of you and should not be interrupted by trivial routines. With our third baby we had a lotus birth where we chose to keep her placenta attached for an extended period of time. This allowed for a spontaneous third stage (the birth of the placenta) but it also meant that she was not able to be weighed or measured until her placenta was cut away. We chose to wait several hours. There was absolutely no reason to rush the 'routine' of measuring and weighing and our beautiful midwife agreed. Do not rush the intimacy of birth, you will never get that time again.

Lastly, take the time to just look at your baby, hold them and touch them. Meeting your baby's needs in the early moments of life makes for a solid and beautiful foundation for communication patterns to develop later.

And remember: all that your baby wants is **you!**

This can be a truly magical feeling, but also the most exhausting and overwhelming of feelings too; trust me, I totally get it having had three babies of my own **but** in the overall scheme of your life and your little ones, they are new to this life for all of three months.

A whole new world of wonder, amazement and a deep, profound love that you never knew existed is opening up before your very eyes. Listen to your intuition, open up your heart space and take the time to connect to your little one. Open yourself up to their teachings because as they grow, so do you.

Natural ways to connect

Breastfeeding

Breastfeeding is a learned art and part of a new lifestyle for both of you as a new mum and your baby. In the early days, you will have moments of wanting to toss out your nursing bras and reach for the feeding bottle. Then comes the realisation that breastfeeding satisfies all three of a newborn babies demands:

"Warmth in the arms of its mother, food from her breasts and security in the knowledge of her presence. Breastfeeding satisfies all three."
Grantly Dick-Read [10]

Why is breastfeeding so good for you and for your baby?

Breastmilk is best for your baby because:

- Breast milk will meet all of your baby's nutritional and hydration needs for the first six months of life.
- Your breast milk will also change throughout a feed, as well as across the months and years to meet your baby's everchanging nutritional immunological as well as developmental needs.
- With regular skin-to-skin contact with you as well as a close interaction throughout your breastfeeding journey, it will only encourage attachment and connection for you both.
- Your breast milk contains so many anti-infective factors that will protect your infant from the illness that's possibly around them.
- Breastfeeding will lower the risk of your infant being overweight, as well as reduce obesity and diabetes in childhood leading into their adulthood.
- Babies who are breastfeeding have better jaw development.
- Lastly, your breast milk will always be far more easily digested than any other milks.

Breastfeeding is best for mother because:

- Early suckling will help to minimise any bleeding after your birth as well as help your uterus return to its pre pregnancy state.
- Breastfeeding will also aid a faster return to your pre-pregnancy body weight because it uses kilojoules to make your milk. How incredible is that!
- Exclusive breastfeeding can delay the return of your fertility (that is only if your infant is breastfeeding every three hours, both day and into the night).
- Breastfeeding can help to reduce the risk of pre-menopausal breast, ovarian and endometrial cancers.
- Lastly, breastfeeding can lead to stronger bones and less osteoporosis for you, mama.

This list is adapted from *Breastfeeding your baby*, New South Wales Department of Health' [11]

Learning to breastfeed takes time, patience and practice. It takes time for you as a new mother as well as your newly born infant to learn the art of breastfeeding. Breastfeeding is not always easy, it is determination, love and much patience.

You do not need to do anything to prepare your breasts for breastfeeding, milk production will develop naturally during your pregnancy. At birth, you will have a thick rich concentrated first milk called 'colostrum.'

"Colostrum is nutritionally rich and provides an immunological boost for your baby's start to life. A hormone is released which signals your breasts to commence making milk. When your baby starts

*suckling, another hormone releases your milk into your milk ducts.
Your milk will flow towards the nipple as your baby suckles. This
is called the 'let down' reflex. Over the next week your milk will
gradually change to become lighter in colour and more abundant.*

*Your breasts will continue to produce milk as your baby suckles.
The more your baby feeds the more milk you will make.*

*In the early weeks and months, you and your baby are getting to
know each other. You will work together to build your milk supply.
By feeding your baby whenever he/she needs it will help get all the
milk he/she needs to grow and develop. When your baby sucks at the
breast, your baby will stimulate tiny nerves in the nipple. This causes
the release of hormones into your bloodstream. One of the hormones
(prolactin) activates the milk making tissues. The other hormone
(oxytocin) causes the breast to push out or let down the milk (the
letdown reflex)."* [12]

Demand = supply: Provided that your baby is correctly attached, the
quickest and most successful way to boost your supply is to breastfeed
more often. Offer a breastfeed every two to three hours during the day
or increase the number of feeds by offering the breast in between your
baby's usual breastfeed.

The more often your baby's sucking causes a letdown, the more
milk is removed from your breast by feeding and in turn more milk
will be made. Always respond to your baby's feeding cues — crying is
a late sign of hunger. Don't limit time at the breast or delay the time
between feeds. A well-drained breast will ensure more milk is made
quickly. Your breasts are never completely empty.

Your baby will stop feeding when they have had enough milk,
while at the same time your breasts are already at work making more
milk. Whatever it is that baby drinks it is automatically replaced, pro-
ducing a constant supply. Your baby will feed often because breast milk

is digested easily and quickly. Your baby's stomach is the size of their clenched fist. So it is common for a young baby to feed eight to 12 times in a 24-hour period, some of which will be at night.

Your breast milk will change throughout the feed; early in the feed the milk will have a lower fat content, which will help to quench the baby's thirst. As the feed goes on, the fat content of the milk rises, which then satisfies the baby's hunger.

A baby allowed to finish the first breast, so that they feed until they come off by themselves before being offered the second breast, will receive the higher fat milk. Your baby may be satisfied with one breast but at other times may want a second or even a third. By switching which breast your baby feeds from first you will ensure each breast keeps making a good amount of milk.

Breastfeeding is one of the many magical moments of bonding and nurturing that you can provide for your baby. As a mother who has breastfed as well as bottle fed (due to our eldest daughter's severe reflux) I strongly hold the belief that breastfed is best. However, in whichever way you choose to feed and nourish your baby and under what circumstances, there needs to be far less judgement and criticism and more support of our choices, as they are often beyond our control.

We know that breastmilk is natures perfect food. It's magical and empowering. Nevertheless, it is not always that simple. In the end, fed is best.

Infant Massage

For parents and children *touch* is a basic and emotional need and want. It is as vital as food. It has been well documented that when infants and children are deprived of affection and physical contact they suffer from negative signs and symptoms, both physical as well as psychological.

Infant massage from the time your wee one can lift their head up is an incredible and enriching way to provide much needed touch and connection, as well as attachment and love for your little one.

Let's look at some of the benefits of infant massage:

- Reducing crying time is a huge incentive!
- Massage improves sleep and will support and regulate sleeping patterns.
- It is ideal for pre-term infants because touch is a key factor in facilitating attachment.
- Infant massage will also enhance your emotions and improve your mood.
- It will improve any wind, colic, reflux or constipation your infant might be experiencing.
- Infant massage will relieve sinus and chest congestion.
- And boost their immune system.
- It will reduce stress hormone levels in both you and your infant.
- Lastly, among so many benefits, infant massage can also enhance your little ones co-ordination.

Before you even think about using infant massage as a way to connect you need to be sure that you have a pure cold pressed fruit, or vegetable oil, free from pesticides and preferably organic on hand. Oils are easily absorbed into the body's system and infants will tend to put their hands and feet in their mouth hence the recommendation for the above.

Never use peanut oil due to high allergens.

Do not massage an infant if they have any open or weeping wounds, infected skin irritations, a fracture or any other acute injuries.

Do not massage your infant if they are bleeding, or have any symptoms of burns including sunburn, and be careful not to massage over an unhealed naval, or any undiagnosed lumps.

There must be **no** abdominal massage if your baby has the hiccups or has just been fed.

This is a great checklist to use before a massage:

- Is it good for you? Are you relaxed?
- Is it good for your little one?
- Get oil, towel, music etc.
- Remove any jewellery.
- Make sure to dim the lights.
- Make sure your hands are nice and warm.

Make sure to have your baby in the right position before you begin. For newborns, perhaps start with sitting on the couch where they can comfortably lie on a towel between or on your thighs with their head resting on your knees.

For an older baby it is best to massage on the floor, maybe on a change mat or a towel.

Before you begin always ask permission!

Start by rubbing your hands together in front of your baby then holding your hands open and asking them "are you ready for a massage?" I know it sounds funny at first but with their body language you will know if it's a yes or no answer. 'Yes' cues may be laying down with a relaxed posture, good eye contact, smiling, cooing, or pulling your hands toward them. A 'no' answer may be a frown with a facial grimace, crying or fussiness, rubbing eyes (too tired) arching their back, avoiding any eye contact, or pushing your hands away.

When you receive a positive response it will be best to start with your baby's legs, with long firm strokes. Place the pads of your fingers on part of your baby's thigh and make circular movements then move to the next place on your little one's legs, and repeat. Avoid the knee and shin area. Next, you might start drawing lines on top of your infant's foot then repeating on the other foot. You might then move to the bottom of your infant's foot and draw one line up then stroke gently down the arch. For your baby's buttocks, cup your hands underneath, and begin to massage using an inward circular motion.

Begin a gentle tummy massage from your left to the right, and always from the side of the belly button across and only just above the belly button to the right.

A simple and gentle massage for the arms and hands is to begin in a circular motion from the shoulder to the wrist, make sure to avoid the elbow.

The above infant massage information has been adapted from the *Baby Massage, Infant Massage Information Service Booklet* (www. infantmassage-imis.com.au).

Connection through touch

Touch and connection are an essential part of your early parenting journey and is beneficial for both of you, it supports an attachment perspective and can help alleviate both from any early signs of depression.

Research has also shown that newborns of depressed mothers may show signs of depression. Based on more then two decades of research, Tiffany Field, director of the Touch Research Institute at the University of Miami Medical School, says that massage therapy (amongst others) are methods that are successfully counteracting the affects of mother's depression on their babies.[13]

Baby-wearing

Throughout many cultures parents wear their babies. Babies who are carried in a variety of cloth type slings or front packs seem to be more content than infants who are kept in cribs, playpens, prams, and plastic seats. Your baby's place in your arms is their expected place.

As Jean Liedloff, author of *The Continuum Concept* [8] says, "What he experiences while he is in arms is acceptable to his continuum, fulfils his current needs, and contributes correctly to his development." Baby-wearing can achieve this. Your infant can be carried in a sling, a wrap or a baby carrier. Perhaps this is due to baby-wearing promoting emotional & mental development.

Author Dr William Sears says on his website

"... in order to help the brain grow and develop, environmental experiences stimulate nerves to branch out and connect with other nerves. Baby wearing helps the infants developing brain to make those right connections. Because baby is intimately involved in their mother and father's world, she is exposed to the environmental stimuli that mum and dad selects, and protected from those sorts of stimuli that bombard and overload her developing nervous system."

Is your baby experiencing a fussy period? Crying and overstimulated? In *The Baby Book* [14] Dr Sears says "Baby wearing parents of previously fussy babies have expressed that their babies are now a joy as their babies are far more content and seem to 'forget to fuss.'"

Baby-wearing also enhances learning. It can help a baby's mental development. Dr Sears notes that studies of carried babies show that these babies do not sleep a lot but actually show an increase in awake contentment time, called 'quiet alertness.' In this state infants are mostly content and able to interact with their environment. Wearing your baby in a safe sling or carrier also creates closeness and helps to establish many emotional and developmental needs. Research has shown that babies cry less, and for babies experiencing reflux, having them upright and near you can help settle them as well as their digestive systems.

Jean Liedloff's expression of an infant in arms is poignant and beautifully written:

> "Every nerve ending under an infant's newly exposed skin will crave the expected embrace, all of his being, the character of all that he is, leads to his being in arms. The violent tearing apart of the mother and child continuum, which is so strongly established in the mother's womb, may understandably result in depression of the mother and agony for the infant." [8]

These precious infant days are an essential time for bonding, nurturing and learning from each other.

Give each other space for this crucial developmental stage. Trust your baby knows what he or she needs and have faith that you, as their parents innately know already. Listen and follow that instinctual calling.

The CARRY Rule of Hand

Baby-wearing is as old as mankind itself. From bark to very basic fabrics, parents across all ages, genres and cultures have developed unique ways of carrying their children mostly out of necessity. Keeping a baby close to them not only kept them warm and safe, but it also freed up a new parents' hands to participate in their everyday chores.

As a matter of survival, many new parents made certain that the supply of life's necessities were never compromised by the arrival of their tribe's newest member.

Baby-wearing offers both functional and emotional benefits. Not only is it convenient, but it also strengthens the bond between parent/caregiver and child. Baby-wearing can also help infants to settle into a deeper sleep as well. Speaking from my own personal experience of baby-wearing, it certainly did!

Modern scientists have recently been able to compute the many and varied benefits of baby-wearing, something that our mothers and fathers before us knew instinctively for many a millennium. Baby-wearing has been proven to not only be a useful parenting tool from supporting an infant with reflux and hip dysplasia, but also prevents any flat head syndrome that may be developing, but baby-wearing will also help to support that healthy emotional attachment that we all wish to attain.

To make safe baby-wearing practices easy to remember, *Babes in Arms* have developed the 'Rule of Hand.' Each finger represents a letter with a different baby-wearing safety tip. By simply learning these five tips, reinforced each time you glance at your hand, you will learn to trust your instincts and enjoy the closeness of your babe.

As a parent, you are ultimately responsible for the safety of your baby, but these tips will give you the confidence you need to wear your baby, and help you to understand safe baby-wearing practices.

> **Careful** If you wouldn't do an activity whilst pregnant, don't do it while you are wearing your baby. Just like being pregnant, baby-wearing can also tilt your centre of gravity and not allow you to be able to see your feet. Make sure to avoid climbing

any ladders, horse riding, parasailing, and or any other risky sport that might lead to a fall. Unlike being inside your womb where the baby is protected to a certain degree, the carried baby will not have that inbuilt protection around them. Be very mindful of what your baby can reach whilst in your carrier. Baby-wearing in the kitchen? Watch out for the hot water in the pot or the kitchen knife when you turn to grab something else!

Airflow You should always be able to see your baby's face easily without needing to open up the fabric of your carrier. Definitely ensure that your baby's chin is not completely pressed up against his/her chest, to allow for easy breathing. To double-check this, slip two fingers underneath your baby's chin to ensure that their breathing is not hindered in any way. If it is, it could lead to 'positional asphyxia.' This can occur in any sort of carrier or wrap, including some prams and car seats that allow your infants head to flop forward. If this happens it can block their very small airways, so be sure to be extra vigilant.

Ride high Keep your baby up high and tight against your chest, not low down on your hips. This will give you a good line of sight so that you can monitor your baby's needs and their wellbeing. A sling or carrier should always mimic how you might hold your baby in your arms, or when back-carrying it will be like giving them a piggy back. You would find it tiring carrying your baby in your arms any lower than your belly button, likewise a sling that will hold your baby this low will quickly prove how to make your back and shoulders very sore!

Right fit Make sure that you have read your sling or carrier instruction booklet thoroughly and perhaps also watch any videos (if available) so that you can ensure that your carrier is the right fit for your body shape as well as the correct one for your baby's age and weight. When you are trying out a new carry position make sure you test it with a doll or a teddy the first few times, perhaps with your partner spot checking you.

Your instinct You are their parent so trust your instinct. Try to mimic with your carrier or sling the way that you would naturally hold your baby within your arms. You should always be able to make eye contact with your baby. This will allow you to determine whether your baby is safe, happy and content. At a glance you should be able to quickly assess if your baby's chin is up and that they are comfortable.

Knowledge is key to your confidence. Remember to research the sling or carrier that you would like to use with your baby and make sure to purchase it from a reputable stockiest. Be sure to seek out help when you need it – the baby-wearing community is incredibly supportive and willing to share any helpful tips they may have. We are blessed in this technological age because it is all literally at your fingertips!

Note: this information has been reproduced in part from *Babes in Arms*. It is intended to provide general information in summary form on the safe use of baby carriers. It does not replace any instructions provided by the manufacturer. *Babes in Arms* and the Australian Breastfeeding Association have said they do not accept liability for any death or injury or damage to property resulting from reliance on this information.[15]

How can I play with my baby?

It is essential to provide your baby with floor play, especially placing your baby on their tummy. And it is never too early to begin reading to your baby. Babies love books. Babies learn and grow rapidly in their first year. Toys and music can help to stimulate their development. Play helps babies learn about their bodies and their world. Many of the interactions you have with your baby are subtle forms of play.

Tummy time

Place your baby on their tummy, on a rug on the floor and place a small brightly coloured toy in front of your baby, so your baby can see it. Some babies don't like to be on their tummy and will protest. It helps to reassure your baby if you get down to floor level with him/her.

Start with a few minutes and gradually increase the time. Talk to your baby to reassure him/her, especially if this is the first few times on their tummy.

Never, ever, leave your baby alone on their tummy.

Why is tummy time important?

Benefits of supervised tummy time for babies include strengthening of his/her neck, shoulder, arm and back muscles (they use these muscles to move around), being able to see the world from different angles, which helps brain development and the time away from resting on the back of the head helps prevent developing a flat spot on his or her head.

You can begin offering supervised tummy playtime as soon as your baby is born, making sure your baby is awake and not too tired, you can offer tummy time at least three times a day.

In the beginning your baby might be a little unsettled and only able to stay on their tummy for a minute or two during playtime. That's okay. There are a few ways to achieve tummy playtime, such as carrying your baby over your arm, shoulder, or chest (only while you are awake) or even on your lap. Tummy time play can also be on the floor, where your baby can play on a comfortable firm mattress or bunny rug.

Using a rolled up towel or nappy under your baby's armpit and chest will give baby a little more support (make sure to remove rolls before baby is placed to sleep on their back). Baby can lift up their head more easily if they are propped up on their elbows too. (See also https://rednose.com.au/article/tummy-time-is-good-for-baby-because)

Reading to your baby

Babies love books. They provide plenty of opportunities for you to tell stories by using descriptive language. Remember to position your baby so he/she can see your face as you read.

Your baby adores your face! Use your voice for different characters and have fun.

Music

Playing music and making music with your baby, is a very positive, interactive, and enjoyable way to play together and key to supporting your baby's development. You can start by singing nursery rhymes and maybe throw in some actions. Move to the rhythm of the music and dance with your baby. Let the music lead you.

As your baby grows, one of their favourite ways to play will probably be by making music, by banging on a saucepan with a wooden spoon or maybe even a toy drum.

Top Tips

You're the best play object your baby can have!

Very young babies enjoy looking at toys and objects with distinct colours – red, black and white. They particularly like objects that have faces on them or checks and stripes. Activity begins for a baby as soon as they respond to light and focus on objects. Having a good visual with light and bright colours is especially important to them.

> **Four months old** Your baby at 16 weeks old will spend much of their waking time in physical activity. He will be able to grasp objects, and enjoy brightly coloured dangling toys.

> **Seven months old** At this age your baby will be playing with their feet and hands and enjoy a lot of vigorous bouncing and kicking. She will love to play with string, paper, soft rubber squeaky toys, rattles, and blocks with balls or beads inside.

> **10 months old** Vocalisation will play a big part of your baby's activity at this stage. He is usually capable of producing two syllable sounds and will enjoy making lip noises and vocalising at a high pitch. They will concentrate on inspection and explore toys by chewing almost everything within reach!

One year old Your baby will now be attempting to pull himself up to stand, he will enjoy cruising, creeping on the floors, and standing up alone. Activities that are enjoyed now, are gross motor activities, such as putting objects in and out of cups, baskets and boxes. Boxes, blocks, rubber and plastic, peg boards and pegs are all fantastic tools for play.

18 months old Your growing child will explore more; they will like stuffed animals; pull toys; and pictures of familiar objects; she will like interesting sounds; and like to participate in routine household activities. He will love to move things around and climb up on anything he can pull himself up on. Play is still quite solitary, so pull toys, push toys, blocks, wooden trains and boxes will all play a role in their activities of play every day.

5

'Becoming' mum

EARLY MOTHERHOOD is particularly brilliant at stripping you of sleep, loading you with mountains of laundry, and have you staring into your third cup of cold coffee wandering if you'll ever get to enjoy it whilst your new baby suckles at your breast for what seems like the umpteenth time in an hour.

Those initial days — weeks and months where hours meld into days and you catch the sunrise more often then you ever envisioned — is a time in your life that feels unending but it is definitely a fleeting moment in time amongst the scheme of a lifetime with your growing children. Infancy is but a year or two and then it's gone only to hold rapture within your memory and heart space.

The *Serenity Prayer* was always something I would hold onto throughout that vulnerable time: "God, grant me the serenity to change the things I can. To accept the things I cannot. Courage to change the things I can; and wisdom to know the difference."

Change is an ever-present feeling throughout your new journey as a parent. Change for me was about 'becoming.' Throughout the early months of being a mother I truly felt my intuitive knowing become stronger and I was truly becoming more of who I already was and 'unbecoming' in so many ways from all that I had been.

'Becoming' mum is the single most enlightening experience that I have ever had. It is also an experience that is daunting, especially in the realisation that there are parts of 'you' that you may need to let go. I remember distinctly thinking that the 'single' Nikki would no longer exist and if the 'single' Nikki no longer existed then who was I? I didn't know myself as 'mum,' but I did know that the baby I held, I loved and that I would reach for the moon and the stars if that would make her happy. I feel that with time I was able to embrace myself as a new mum but I was also able to gather the pieces of my 'old' self and reclaim them again, but that also took time.

Those 'old' pieces of self become an identity for us and it can be very hard to let it go. As time continued, those parts of me I realised were different. They held a different meaning. The 'single' Nikki hadn't actually been single for a very long time but I did yearn to go out with my girlfriends, to drink wine, talk and dance all night long again. As our daughter grew and I felt comfortable in leaving her I did exactly that. It was fun sure, but it was never the same. I just wasn't the same. It took me years to come to that realisation.

When we are sifting through the pieces of ourselves, that we have moved on from, a beautiful exercise for me was to just sit with it. I would journal those feelings and sit in reflection for a while. Whatever feelings came up I would acknowledge them and then let them go. Sometimes feelings would come up that I would suddenly long for or struggle to let go of, or my girlfriends were going out and I had a sick baby or maybe a clingy one.

Again, I would sit with it, journal about it, gather up those feelings and thoughts and think about whether I really did want to feel like that or do I really want to go out or am I actually just content being here in this moment whilst sitting with my baby in my arms?

Some of our past thoughts and feelings are definitely in the past and it is always so beautiful to look back upon them with love and fondness. But are you that person still? Do you even want to be?

Early motherhood is a completely new chapter, an evolving one, one that unravels you and changes you in ways that are indescribable and it's okay to not be the same person that you were, perhaps even just a week ago.

The beginnings of motherhood is only for a season. This season into motherhood with a new baby will in fact be your shortest but you will feel the intensity of it right down deep into your very bones. This season is short, yes, but the changes of self are intense. You will experience lows that you have never felt before and feelings of overwhelm will creep up on you when you least expect it. You are learning, your new baby is learning. Time will be your greatest teacher, so sit in knowing that you are strong, and you are more than capable to be here to be the mama that your baby has chosen.

There is no doubt that having a new baby feels a lot like *Groundhog Day*. It can be relentless, with numerous nappy changes, feeding, burping, mopping up spat-out milk and changing clothes (again!), long nights and no privacy anymore, you will find yourself showering with a baby sitting in their bouncer watching you. You will go to the toilet with a baby on your lap and at times you might even feel a little, dare I say it, bored.

Those feelings are all okay. These are all normal feelings and frustrations and it doesn't mean that you don't love your baby. It may even mean that you miss the past you, the you that had copious amounts of freedom, a career that you love/ed, friends to sip wine and coffee with whenever you felt the urge. It's difficult to make those plans now, you are always late, some days you are much too tired to even get out of your pyjamas, some mornings you wake up curled in a ball crying from the loss of sleep you'd experienced the night before, the loss of self that you want back.

Again, these are normal feelings; feelings that you need to lean into, feelings that you need to have so that you can move forward into the day that is still yet to come.

I want you to know that I felt **all** those feelings too and some. I thought that I mustn't love my new baby due to all of these intense feelings. I didn't have anyone there to tell me that what I was feeling was normal because, I didn't talk about it. I didn't know how to. Indeed, I felt that if I **did** speak my truth my husband, friends and family would think that I didn't love our new baby, that they would think me as a horrible, ungrateful mum and that I should be happy to have a healthy baby.

I didn't know then that feeling lonely and longing for the past me was okay. In fact it is absolutely normal. I didn't know then that everything would be okay, that those feelings would pass with time and that I would and did settle into a new kind of normal, motherhood. I felt the love I had for my daughter within the deepest parts of me.

I hated motherhood in those early days post-partum, I wondered what I was doing what was I thinking when I thought I could be a mum, I would think to myself "I can't do this!"

But I did do it. My husband did eventually find out how I was feeling, and he loved me through it, without judgement, because at that point I had stopped internalising how I was feeling. I had stopped judging myself.

We will **all** go through the ebbs and flows of new motherhood. Every single birth will be unique as will the baby you've brought Earthside. You will need space to process and sift through it all. 'Becoming' mum will change and evolve with every baby that you have. If you can practice non-judgement and self-compassion now, then those flows will weave through your life and make every unique transition a little easier.

When we can practice the art of self-compassion we are in fact encountering ourselves. This can be overwhelming and also a little confronting. We are looking at ourselves and seeing our daily struggles. After gazing into the mirror and seeing your swollen eyes caused by crying for hours. Know that it is okay. These moments of anger, sadness, loss and loneliness don't define you. Your emotions are not the definition of who you are as a person or as a parent. Forgive yourself and let it go.

How we choose to live our own lives can sometimes be our best teachers. When we are kind to ourselves we unknowingly give ourselves permission to be warm and kinder to our own children, it is almost like we are 'reparenting' ourselves with a self-compassionate state of being.

Circling back, **change** can be overpowering. The feelings and emotions that come up almost on a daily basis can be unremitting. Please speak up, use your voice and speak your truth, there is no shame in feeling the way that you do, at varied stages during motherhood we all feel swept up and away from the landslide of change both within and inside our homes.

Begin slowly as you unpeel the many layers, starting with someone you trust, confiding in them because you know there will be no judgement and if there is no one around you like that, it's okay to call someone professional for support. Resources include *Beyond Blue* (www.beyondblue.com.au) and COPE for guidance and support.

We need to start the process of normalising these new motherhood *feels*. We need to support one another and acknowledge the many changes that we each experience. If we can't do this as a collective we can certainly do it as individuals or within our homes. Speaking our truth will enable us all as new mothers and as women to gently ease through each motherhood transition with much more grace, with more loving kindness for each other and ourselves. Only then can we start to embrace the new parts of ourselves that we didn't even know existed until now.

Motherhood creates a whole other worldly dimension of being a human being. You will become more *present*. Time will stand still for you with a new baby in arms, and nothing other than your new family will matter anymore. You will no longer be focused on what is around you or what is happening on your social media channels because all you will want right now is what is within that moment, the one where you are holding your new baby. There is nothing quite like that sense of contentment.

Change, not struggle

Change is different for everyone. Some people love it and embrace it. Others (like me) struggle against its tide. When our first baby was born, I couldn't quite get my head around how correct the feeling of *Groundhog Day* was. Every day felt the same. Awake at five am, breastfeed, change baby's nappy, breastfeed again. Shower, get baby changed, change nappy again and breastfeed. Put baby down for a nap, make my breakfast. Baby wakes up, change nappy, breastfeed. Play with baby, breastfeed, then put baby down for another nap. Make a cup of tea, put on laundry, make my lunch, baby wakes up. Change nappy, breastfeed, play with baby, breastfeed, change nappy again. Somehow cook dinner with baby in my arms or on the boob, husband home, he plays with baby while I run the bath. Bath baby, get baby dressed, breastfeed baby to sleep. Dinner time, breastfeed baby again then sleep. Wake up the next day and repeat.

Motherhood for me became an all-encompassing process of 'becoming' mum. It didn't feel good to me it felt a lot like it was happening 'to me' and that it was all out of my control. It felt like I was watching from another realm and I saw myself and how sad I was slowly becoming. It was overwhelming.

As our baby grew, due to being on repeat for the last few months, I couldn't quite fathom how to go with the ebbs and flows as she changed. Dramatically changed. Teething kicked in, sleep regressions, solid food started and she was on the move, change was definitely, once again, on the way. Change can be much like a metamorphosis especially when you become parents.

It is a whole new way of being and it transforms you in ways you never knew existed. The capacity for change when you become parents is vast because in a lot of ways, you really have no choice, yet it just happens. If nothing else. the best take away I can ask you to grasp is that, change is **not** happening **to** you, it is happening **through** you. We are energy and it is always moving and shifting therefore early motherhood and all of it's overwhelm will move on too.

Again, I felt that I was becoming less of who I once was, but I didn't know where I was heading. I was butting up against myself and the changes that were 'happening to me' were frustrating and I didn't know how to make myself happy outside of being a mum anymore.

It was around the ten months mark post-partum, after we'd been forced to move into my parents' home due to my husband losing his job, I was put into a position that I hadn't planned, going back to work. It was not long after I was found naked nursing my baby and sitting on the bathroom floor hysterical and unsure of how to even get myself up. I knew then that only I could pull myself up out of the depths of my own darkness.

With time, a lot of emotional support from my husband and trust in myself again as Nikki, not just as being a mum, I realised that change can in fact be embraced rather than feared. It is about trusting in life's transitions and surrendering to it rather than fighting the growth that will inevitably always take place.

When we allow change to shift and flow rather than letting it fill you up until you're so overwhelmed you feel lost, is when you will start to become more present, life will begin to slow down to a pace that finally feels right for you. You will feel more aware and present in your body and your emotions, and you will be more in your own power then you thought was ever possible.

When you feel more in your authentic power you can then begin to set up healthy boundaries with those with whom you share your life, you will know who to surround yourself with and with who no longer lights you up. It is okay to set yourself healthy boundaries — in fact, it is essential.

Your capacity to mother changes all the time. You are mother once you conceive, then birth and nurture your baby with your breast. Mothering changes again when you move onto solids and then baby-led weaning. You are mother once the need for your own space happens, baby from bassinet to cot to their own room. Motherhood changes constantly whilst nurturing your baby throughout their every *first*: their first time sitting, crawling and walking, their first word, sentence and sleep through the night. You are mother as you watch them grow, when you realise that you have grown too, grown in spirit, intuitiveness and in self.

You are mother through all these many and varied challenges with many more to come. These changes represent your energy flowing and moving. Motherhood is happening through you and it is so beautiful to sit back and watch how it flourishes for you both.

'Becoming' mum is an all-encompassing feeling. It will create many varied changes in your life but most importantly within you. These changes will continue to evolve as time goes on and as your baby grows so will you too.

Welcoming-in change

Mindfulness: for your mind

Mindfulness can come in many forms but I like to think of it in regards to this new journey you are on as *Mindful Parenting.*

Mindful parenting is an essential part of being a parent: it is a lifelong practice. A practice that will take you to the centre of what *peace* is for you. With time you will find yourself feeling less agitated about little things that you would have genuinely been upset about. It will keep you focusing on the present moment and it will create a sense of calm within you.

Mindful parenting is about becoming less attached to the outcome and more mindful of what is unfolding in yours and your children's lives.

Some core characteristics of mindfulness include the following:

Observation

Being mindful aims to shift your focus of attention away from thinking to simply observing, observing your thoughts, feelings and all of the many sensations around you.

Being non-judgemental

This is an important aspect to adopt as we all can relate to trying to control what we're experiencing at times. When being mindful no attempt is made in evaluating your experience or to say 'that it is good, bad or terrible, right, wrong, or a failure.'

This can take some time to develop because accepting all of your experiences can be a challenge, but by bringing about a kind, gentle curiosity to your experience it can become a very simple way of creating a sense of non-judgement.

For example: you're at a park breastfeeding your new baby in public. You're watching your toddler play and haven't noticed the woman across from the park staring at you. You can feel eyes on you, you look around and catch the woman's eye. She looks straight at you and shakes her head, as if in disgust that you are breastfeeding your baby without so much of a cover, in a public place.

Now, you can take this personally and turn around with tears in your eye, or you can look straight into the eyes of this lady and smile. Knowing that this is her reaction and only she is responsible for those feelings of disgust that have come up for her. You can be mindful of the fact that this is one of those 'experiences' that need no judgement and carry on breastfeeding your beautiful and hungry new baby whilst watching the joy on your toddler's face as they play with their tip truck in the sand.

This takes patience and time, but in practicing non judgement of our daily experiences will always take us to a place of calm.

Focus on one thing at a time — being present

We live in a fast-paced world and with a young infant there can be so many different variables, breastfeeding every two to three hours, constant nappy changes, meeting your baby's varied needs, your baby wanting and needing attention, as well as affection, laundry piling up, meals to be prepared and cooked, other young children to take care of, cleaning, daily activities, maintaining friendships with coffee dates, quality time with your partner, grocery shopping, the gym. You might even be working amongst all of this. Throw it altogether and life can seem more than a little overwhelming.

Being **present** will take ongoing practice. When you sense you're drifting away from either the task at hand, or you're playing with your baby but whilst doing so you're also thinking about the dishes that need to be done, or ogling the sandwich and coffee yet to be consumed. Observe those thoughts, and let them drift away. Refocus on your baby, their giggling coos and sweet smiling face, stay present, because your future you will thank you!

The early days of being a parent can be exhausting. Start your day by taking three deep mindful breaths. Do this throughout your day to help ground yourself in the present moment. Deep breathing is an amazing tool to keep you physically well and calm.

According to Dr Libby Weaver in her book *Rushing Woman's Syndrome,* [16] your breath dominates your autonomic nervous system. It does this because your breath is the only part of the autonomic nervous system that you can control consciously. Dr Weaver says: 'the role of the autonomic nervous system is to perceive the internal environment and after processing the information in the central nervous system, regulate the function of your internal environment.' (p. 119) In a nutshell, your breath leads and therefore your body follows.

Did you know that we breathe five thousand to 30 thousand times daily? Every. Single. Day.

Breathing has the power to influence your body positively in many ways! It communicates to your body that you are safe when you are breathing calmly and deeply, or it can communicate to your body that you are not when you are breathing shallow and short.

Pencil in ten minutes for yourself for this simple exercise. Grab a comfortable cushion on the floor in a room where you won't be interrupted. To start, sit comfortably with your hand placed gently on your belly. Breathe softly and deeply, focusing on your breath and expanding your ribs or belly as much as possible. Hold your breath for a few seconds, then let it go for two seconds longer than your inhaled breath. You are helping your body shift from a state of arousal and stress to one of calm and relaxation. This can also be a good practice whilst breastfeeding or even when soothing your unsettled baby.

Another beautiful way to ground yourself at the start of your day is to create a 'ritual.' It can be whilst your baby or toddler are playing, or maybe your baby is sleeping. Make yourself a tea, coffee, or warm water with lemon. Grab your journal or a notebook and begin by starting a gratitude list. This can be as simple as starting with "I am thankful today for ... coffee, sleeping baby, no tantrums from my little one (yet) etc.

This allows your day to start with a positive mindset, one that is grateful and calm, as well as a feeling of being grounded within your unique present moment.

Journaling Prompts

As parents it is so important to do something to keep your mind fresh, and weave positive patterns within your life.

Journaling allows you to move through your emotions rather than to dwell on them. It allows you the space to feel more positive emotions, relish beautiful experiences, and build upon the negative aspects through the written word rather than siting on it and remaining in that mindset.

Journaling can truly be a recipe for a happier life. Researchers have found that people who *write* about *gratitude* are more optimistic and feel better about their lives in general.

Morning
* Write down three things you are grateful for.
* What would make today great?
* Daily affirmations or mantras eg. 'I am'

Afternoon
* Three amazing things that happened today.
* How could I have made today better?

I also like to look at daily quotes or affirmations that I relate to and either write them out or dive into the quote or affirmation to nut out why I resonate with it at that time in my life.

Journaling for me is a space where I can write out my true feelings, regain my true self. I will sometimes meditate and then journal about what's come up for me while I meditated. I feel that it's a great space to talk to myself, to write letters that may or may not be read, and to authentically pour my heart out and rage on topics that I might not otherwise have talked about.

My sincerest hope for you is that journaling can become a much-loved part of your life too: "Journaling is like whispering to one's self and listening at the same time." (Mina Murray)

Gratitude lists

A gratitude list is the beginning of self-empowerment. It is the creation of a 'positive thoughts list' and the start of focusing on what you have to be thankful for. Look for things that create a stirring in your soul, what makes **you** happy? It can be as simple as a cup of tea, or putting some makeup on in the morning!

Create some space in those first precious weeks post-partum to make a list of things that make your heart happy, that make *you* **you**. In amongst the beauty of the newborn haze we tend to forget ourselves a little. This list is a good reminder of who you are as well as being a 'mum.'

Put your 'Gratitude/Self-Care' list somewhere that you look at regularly, and make it as pretty or inspiring as you would like. Remember take a break every day, if only for 10 minutes, to create some space for you. Here are some ideas:

• A 10 minute meditation.
• Watch your favourite TV show.
• Pour a cuppa, put your feet up and *breathe*.
• An afternoon bath with rose petals and your favourite smells.
• Snuggle up in your favourite spot with a good book.
• Have a delicious nap!

The best time can often be when your baby sleeps, so remember, 10 minutes for *you*. You will feel recharged, revitalised, & rejuvenated!

Walking meditation

Another form of mindfulness is a *walking meditation*. It is a simple practice for developing a sense of calm and connectedness. It can be practiced at any time of the day. It's a perfect meditation to practice for those middle of the night wakings with an unsettled infant. Practice your three mindful breaths whilst you walk.

Continue those deep, full present breaths, direct your attention to your feet planted firmly on the ground, then take a step, feeling the weight distribution under your feet. Notice the feeling of your muscles holding both you and your baby up, letting go of any unnecessary tension and then begin to walk slowly, with full attention to your body and breath. Whenever your attention wanders, take your three mindful breaths and begin again to reconnect with your body whilst you move.

This sort of meditation can be done anytime. Walking around the block in the 'witching hour' with your unsettled infant, a beautiful beach walk — the list goes on.

Mindfulness is a beautiful practice to adopt and develop. It takes time and patience to create a routine around parenting little ones but it continues to be a simple and effective practice that helps to create calm within yourself and your home. As I always like to say: 'your calm is their calm!'

6

Conscious Parenting

BEFORE OUR first daughter was born my husband and I didn't discuss how we would raise our children. We didn't know anything about co-sleeping or baby wearing, in fact we didn't even realise it was a 'thing,' let alone have it cross our minds to even do it once Ashta was here.

Antenatal classes went into the depths of the clinical ways of birthing — for example, a tour of the birthing ward, what the resuscitation trolley looked like, education on the varied drugs to ask for in childbirth and then a birth video of a mother birthing in the bed. Our midwife touched on breastfeeding but did not go into the intricacies of demand feeding, the evening cluster feeds to expect or the fact that my nipples would feel like a tiny animal has been nibbling at them until they crack and/or bleed.

The truth is, I went there to socialise and eat from the fresh fruit tray offered. I can honestly say neither myself or my husband were

captured by the classes nor did they excite us enough to do birth research outside of them.

In hindsight we were young and naïve, I knew that to give birth
was to do so vaginally or via a caesarean section, I knew that I wanted
to breastfeed but other than that we were simply clueless, not to men-
tion completely uninspired.

After our daughter was here, and we were in the thick of our
new journey into parenting, my husband and I were like ships in the
night, we were tired, we weren't talking to each other and to be honest
I dreaded asking him how his day was. I envied that he was talking to
adults all day and using his brain. I also knew that I really didn't have
the emotional capacity to hold space for him if he had had a bad day.
I could barely do that for our daughter and I certainly wasn't doing
it for myself. Ben was working long hours and my days were spent
with a new baby who catnapped throughout the day and would feed
relentlessly only to projectile vomit everywhere not long afterwards. I
thought that was normal (FYI: it's not!).

As partners and new parents, we were complete strangers. In fact,
I dreaded him coming home because I was worried he would slam
the door on his way in after having just put Ashta to sleep. Bedtimes
for us would cause me anxiety because the last thing I felt like doing
was going through the motions of foreplay and making love knowing
that within a couple of hours of actually falling asleep I'd be awoken
to hungry cries again, and then every two hours again after putting
her to sleep.

The anxiety I felt, and now know upon reflection and discussion
that he did too, left very little time to discuss what we wanted, how
we felt, and were we even going to move forward as a family. In fact,
sadly there was a time there amongst the mess, and the madness, were

we to even remain together as a couple, a new family? The question on our lips was: is this what marriage with children feels like? This brings me to...

What is Conscious Parenting?

There are many definitions of **conscious parenting**. For me, I believe that *conscious* parenting is about leaning into a deeper understanding of your own childhood and having the emotional capacity to lean further into certain aspects of that journey. There are some aspects of your childhood — and the way that your parents parented you — that you may wish to take along with you on your unique journey. Others, you may wish to leave behind.

Conscious parenting can also be about uncovering specific childhood wounds and or situations or values that you would like to **not** repeat in your own parenting journey. I believe that we are all a product of our childhood unless we decide to change it. What you decide to change and how you go about making that change happen is totally up to you.

An example of a form of punishment that I and many of us from the Generation Y (or Millennials) childhood era were subject to is smacking. There is still a long held belief that smacking works. Have you ever heard someone say "well I was smacked it worked for me, I turned out okay." This is a statement I have heard so many times in my career. I beg to differ, because research has since proven that smacking, in fact, creates anxiety and aggression in later years.

Professor Raymond Arthur, of Northumbria University in the UK wrote about some important research on the consequences of smacking young children:

"Researchers in the US examined over 50 years' of research involving more than 160,000 children and concluded that smacking children does in fact cause more harm than good. The researchers found smacking often 'does the opposite' of what parents want and rarely results in increased immediate compliance by children. It was also shown that children who are smacked are more likely to exhibit higher levels of aggression and mental health problems as they grow up." [17]

Maybe you turned out 'okay,' maybe you did not. The point is it could in fact be something that you and your family will *choose* consciously to not use as a disciplinary tool for your children. You might choose to not repeat patterns and behaviours that you feel may create fear rather than respect.

Another way I choose to define conscious parenting, is to create a conversation. When we as partners decide to raise a family, why don't we sit down and discuss how we want to raise them?

I chose to share our story because I believe that if Ben and I had had at least one discussion about how we would like the birth to be, if we had talked about the post-partum period and what our expectations were, taking into account the loss of sleep and sleeping environments, or whether we would let our baby cry, or whether we had firm views in holding them through it (I know in hindsight that we really did have zero clue) such a conversation may have at least opened those channels of connection and conversation. It wouldn't have been an overwhelming conversation later, even with the sleepless nights because we would have already spoken about it.

These conversations are so important when you are planning a family because once the cat's out of the bag so to speak, everybody has an opinion on everything. Those opinions are usually well meaning but they can become overwhelming. I distinctly remember my mum being a little taken aback by the prospect of us planning a natural birth, and that I wanted to breastfeed.

My mum's experience of birth was an emergency caesarean and bottle feeding me. My parents would both say to me: "oh well, if you can't birth naturally that's okay," or "if you can't breastfeed it's okay to use formula."

I respected that that was their opinion. What I didn't know then though, was that those words crept in from time to time and clawed their way into my subconscious, illuminating all of my doubts and fears. I didn't know as a new and vulnerable mum that because of their experience and the way in which they shared their story that I would subconsciously feel that that would happen to me, too.

What I have learnt since, is that I am not my mum. I was never going to experience birth and post-partum the exact same way that she did, but what I could have taken from that conversation — if my husband and I had previously talked more openly and consciously about things like how we wanted to give birth and experience our post-partum — was for it to open up an important topic for discussion: what were our expectations for the birth? How would we have a gentle post-partum and transition for us as new parents and our baby? And how would we discuss this with our family so that they can better understand and support our choices.

However way you choose to look at it, conscious parenting will always begin with a healthy dose of self-reflection. It begins in your early childhood years and from there you are able to seek the light amongst the shadows.

What I mean by this is dependent on how you grew up, your parents parenting style. Were they permissive parents? Were they dominant or peaceful? These are all aspects of self as a child that now as a parent you need to draw upon. Do you see yourself parenting in a similar way and, if so, is that how you would like to raise your own children?

7

Parenting on the same page

FULL DISCLOSURE: we are **all** new to this parenting gig. It doesn't matter if this is your first, second third or fourth baby, they are all unique and you are different every single time.

But before we delve further into this subject, it is imperative to at least discuss *you*, and your values as a couple, and as parents.

Our babies were not born with a manual explaining everything that we needed to know for them to thrive, nor were we given option A, B, or C regarding how we wanted to parent. All these lessons have developed with time. They've come with experience, and it's also hopefully something you have both discussed. If not, let this be a gentle reminder to do so.

Becoming parents is one of the most exciting, incredible times of our lives, it can also be the most humbling. It is no longer about us anymore, it is suddenly about keeping alive this little human that we have been blessed with.

This transition into parenting isn't going to be a relatively easy one if you're not on the same page. It comes down to the values you wish to instil as a family. How you hope to teach your children right from wrong, and something as simple as sleep can and will very quickly become the cause of much distress within your home and as parents, especially if you both have differing views. For example, one might prefer crying it out, whereas the other leans more into a gentle way to settle your little one into dreamland. I implore you if you haven't, to take the time to discuss it.

Countless times I have heard from parents that they just can't agree on things to do with their kids. Common examples include dinner times: *Mum*: "Honey if you eat a little more dinner you can have some fruit afterwards"; *Dad*: "No way, we can't offer dessert up if they haven't eaten all of their dinner." Another example: *Mum*: 'I don't' want to smack our kids;' *Dad*: 'Well I was flogged, and I turned out okay!'

Yes, I have made dad seem like the 'tough guy,' but more often than not though that is the case. Perhaps that's because of the generation where tough love was key, and boys weren't encouraged to show emotion. An important philosophy that I like to teach is emotion regulation, including and especially as parents. Because responsible modelling starts with us.

Dr John Gottman of the Gottman Institute is an internationally respected marriage and relationships researcher and expert. He estimates that close to 70 percent of what we *don't* like about our partner will never change. It's difficult to shift habits; expectations of other people are a challenge and some things are just a part of who we are.

Hearing from someone that you love that you're doing it all wrong isn't going to go down so well. How would you feel if your loved one said: "Hey Hun, I think you're parenting all wrong here." I don't think you'll be smiling, nodding your head in agreement and saying "Actually babe you're right, I'm parenting terribly."

People don't like to be 'fixed,' nor do they like being told that they're wrong. While we all want to do the best that we can with the knowledge that we got most of the know-how that we **do** have from our own parents parenting us. If your partner thinks that "they turned out all right," despite being flogged than they're not going to take lightly you trying to 'fix' their parenting style. In fact, they might take it as you suggesting *his* parents are wrong, which in turn will make him feel like you think he's turned out 'wrong' too.

Parenting is a personal journey and this belief that we are condemned to continue down the same path as our parents leaves very little room for growth within the current generation of parents, if we allow that to be our thought process.

When our second daughter was born my maternity leave at that time around ran out at around the six months mark. I was still breastfeeding but had no other choice then to go back to work. We decided on weekend work so that my husband could have the girls as I wasn't yet ready for our baby to be in a childcare centre. This meant that he would have the girls from seven am until three pm with a lunchtime feed in between. Ben would drive to my workplace so I could breastfeed our daughter on my lunch break because I couldn't get a lot of milk out when pumping.

My husband was the sole carer at home over the weekends and this meant that I had to trust that he would parent them gently, consciously and with an attachment view in mind. Not only that, but I also needed to 'let go.' I needed to allow him the space to parent his way. This was slow learning for me and — I won't lie — there were plenty of times I came home and the house looked like a bomb had hit it: dirty nappies piled up, dishes in the sink and the kids were still in their pyjamas **but** they had built a cubby house in the lounge room, and they were fed, clothed and so happy.

This kind of trust for me and many parents came because of sitting down and discussing our values around how we'd like to be parenting. Topics such as: would we smack our kids (full disclosure, I was smacked when I was a kid, I'd like to think I turned out okay but regardless, I don't think it's any type of answer when we resort to violence); would we yell at our kids; co-sleep; breastfeed, would we use cloth nappies or disposable? The list goes on.

The simple fact is, from experience, this worked for us because we'd discussed it and we trusted each other because we'd talked it through thoroughly beforehand.

In the end, we are not all perfect people, but we can at least try to agree on some things, acceptance of each other parenting differently but with the same approach is always a sense of unity as far as relationships and parenting go.

The guide below will hopefully give you an opportunity to sit down to talk and agree on how you can get on the same page. I always feel it's best to start with the positive things that you like about each other!

Set a time to sit with a bottle of wine or cup of tea and discuss the things that strengthen you.

- What is one thing that your partner does with your children that you love?
- How can this be a bigger part of your days together?
- What are three things that you like to do together as a family?
- How can you create time for more of those things?

When we focus on the positive things that you like to do together as a family it will always leave more room for alignment and connection rather than focusing on the negative.

The next focus task is to look at creating the same vision that you both see moving forward as a family.

- Do you have a vision of what you would like your family to feel like? I say *feel*, because we all wish to feel a certain way, we want to feel happy, for an example so how can we create happy in our home as a family, together?
- Consistency is key, but consistency with the right things for your family.
- What do you value most within your home?
- When our child challenges us do we want a hard approach a soft approach or a gentle but firm approach?
- What do we want our children to feel from us? Again, I say feel because I want you to think about feelings, do you want your child to feel anger or happiness when they are communicating with you?
- If there is unacceptable behaviour how best can we communicate what we want in a way that fits in with the above answers?
- What can we put in place right now, together, to move forward?

Getting on the same page won't always be easy. You might not even agree to getting on the same page. If this is the case perhaps you can look into experimenting with your varied styles of parenting, for example for a few days try your partner's approach (only if it is safe and it feels okay for you both), then switch back to your approach and see which feels best for the whole family.

An important point I'd like to make here is to agree not to fight about this in front of your kids. Do it privately so you can ensure you are not undermining one another in front of your children. This then at least promotes respectful communication. Sometimes, professional help is what's needed and that's okay too.

Lastly, I suggest a ... date night.

When we are able to sift through a couple of different things to get onto the same page it will lighten the load that parenting can bring when we aren't in agreement.

Working together to parent consciously

Let's start with savouring your successes. Every night grab yourself a cup of tea and a special notebook that you've purchased or made for your 'gratitude' lists and add another section. You are going to write down at least **three** things that went well that day. List the big and the small things and savour them, then enjoy them and give yourself a **big** hug!

You are also going to pencil in **date nights**! It doesn't have to be *out*, it can be at home. Once the kids are in bed you can cook up a much-loved meal together or order in a take-away, with a beverage of choice and *talk*! All devices are off, and you are both switching off to reconnect with each other.

Let's start with three date nights. For my husband and I we have a home date night every Friday. All devices are off, as we chat he makes me dinner, we share a bottle of wine and then we might watch a movie on *Netflix*. We need and look forward to it!

Date night: how can we be more present in our children's lives?

Some suggested topics of discussion:

- How can we play more?
- Can we organise annual holidays/OR can we organise one more day off on either side of a couple of long weekends throughout the year?
- In what ways or how can we show that we love them (apart from the obvious example — telling them "I love you."
- How can we set aside at least one day if not two, every week to spend an entire day switched off from everything and just 'being' together?
- How can we help each other to achieve this?

Date night: what can we do for each other?

- Talk about at least two things that will help each other in your daily lives, for example, could your partner fold the laundry?
- Talk about at least two things that will recreate space for you both to enjoy something you love individually. For example, she might love shopping or reading a book, he might love bike riding or surfing. How can you create space for you to both find time for your own unique loves?

It is important when raising a family that you realise you are also raising yourselves, both as individuals, as a couple and as parents. How can you create space for you to both grow together as a couple and as parents as well as evolve as individuals?

How can you create space to parent on the same page?

And how can you both help each other to carve out the space as individuals to pursue what you love? Here is some food for thought for a series of date nights to come (I hope!).

Possible topics of discussion:
- What are your favourite childhood memories?
- How would you like your children to remember their childhoods?
- What can you do to make it a memorable one? Ideas are, camping, beach days, picnics at the park.

In the next chapter I will describe four different parenting styles for you so you can discern which one was your parent's unique style and perhaps you'll also see some truth for your own. Perhaps it's something that hasn't completely resonated with you or 'felt' right, so this is an opportunity to look at the reasons why and what you could possibly change.

❧ 8 ❧

Parenting styles

T HERE ARE FOUR basic parenting styles identified by the Gottman institute. Most of you will use a mix of these styles when it comes to your parenting, but one style will usually be the dominant one and will, therefore, have the greatest impact on your child.

In order to be authentic in the way you consciously raise your child you need to be honest with yourself about your parenting style so that you can move forward on your conscious parenting journey.

Emotion coach style

These parents will base their parenting style on teaching and redirecting their child to learn more about their emotions. They will:

• See that their child's emotions are a perfect time for connection and reconnection.

• Validate their child's emotions.

- Make sure they carve out time to stop and always connect with their child to discuss any feelings that have come to surface.
- Always try to go deeper into why their child is feeling the way that they do.
- Will help their child become more aware of their feelings by labelling them and allowing them the space to express their feelings rather than help them repress them.
- Express empathy and seek out connection.
- Tend to avoid criticising or labeling their feelings as stupid, shy, silly, ridiculous etc in front of their child.
- Will tend to remain calm whilst also helping their child solve the problem at hand.
- Lastly, they are more aware of their own emotions as a parent and also as a human being.

Within this realm of parenting, your toddler will learn to trust their own feelings, regulate their emotions and begin to solve their own problems. Your toddler may develop high self-esteem, learn well and begin to get along with others.

Permissive style

If you practice this parenting style you:

- Will accept your child's emotions but will not tend to help your child better understand their emotions.
- Will show empathy.
- Be unable to use your child's emotions for problem solving.
- May struggle to set limits and have boundaries.
- May believe that there is very little that you can do with your

child's negative emotions other than for them to just 'ride them out.'

- May have a 'hands off' idea about handling your child's emotions, meaning that you may struggle to help your child name their emotions.
- As parents can help your child by showing and expressing your own emotions but you may have a difficult time processing them.

Your toddler may struggle to learn how best to regulate their emotions. They might even have trouble concentrating, forming friendships, and getting along well with others, especially when they are in an emotional state.

Dismissive style

This parenting style means you might:

- Find yourself ignoring your child's feelings.
- Believe that it is more important to always have a positive mindset and to not dwell on any negative emotions.
- Find it difficult to be around your child when they are feeling sad, angry, scared or hurt, any negative emotions may be uncomfortable for you.
- Use distraction on a regular basis to assist in dealing with your child's emotions.
- Find yourself dismissing your child's emotions as part of them 'just being a kid' or them 'not really understanding.'
- Find yourself dismissing feelings of sadness, and aim to control or bottle up your own anger.
- Also find it hard showing your feelings.

Your child might come to the belief that their own feelings are wrong, or not valid. Your child might also think that there is something deeply wrong with them because of the way that they feel. They might even have a very difficult time in regulating their emotions.

Disapproving style

Parents with this parenting style might:

- Judge and also criticise your child's emotions.
- Try to set limits upon your child's emotional expression and how long they can 'feel' that way.
- View your child's emotions as a behaviour that needs to be controlled, something they should not be expressing.
- View your child's sadness as 'your child getting their own way' or being manipulative.
- Also disapprove of any feelings of anger.
- Believe that any negative emotions are a bad part of people.
- Have the belief that in showing your emotions it makes you weak, and that children must be tough in order to survive in this world.
- Not feel comfortable or perhaps haven't been shown how to express your emotions unless you're very angry or depressed.

Like the children of parents who use a dismissive style of parenting, the children of parents who are *disapproving* might come back to that same belief that their feelings are wrong, and definitely not valid. They might even feel that something is wrong with them because of the way that they feel. Your toddler might also have great difficulty in regulating their emotions. (Adapted from The Gottman Institute: https://www.gottman.com/blog/the-four-parenting-styles/)

❧ 9 ❧

Temperament

TEMPERAMENT IS another important aspect we as parents need to understand better. It is something that we are born with, a set of traits that will make each of us unique — and it's a powerful factor in defining how we react to the world around us.

Tie this in with your own parenting style and it might be that the way you are parenting your little one does not quite gel with *their* temperament. Parents need to understand is that they cannot change who they innately are, but you can change aspects of yourself and how you parent so that you can better support your child within their foundation years.

Personality Traits

As soon as your toddler reaches the ripe age of two, he will begin to show a particular type of personality. The most familiar type at this age will be active, outgoing, self-focused **and** full of curiosity.

Then between the ages of two to five years your child may tend to develop more of an altered personality dependent on their own unique nature as well as the home environment in which they are raised.

Extraversion

As a parent you might find yourself referring to your toddler "as a firecracker." This can be due to the type of personality that he has, a child with an exuberant amount of energy. These children will be active, assertive, outgoing, and very talkative.

Agreeableness

These little people will tend to interact with great warmth and compassion. They will be incredibly affectionate, forgiving, generous, kind and also empathetic.

Openness/Intellect

You might find that your toddler will display depth and a very real imagination. They will be artistic, very curious, imaginative, and have an array of different interests.

Conscientiousness

This particular trait is more about your toddlers' impulse control. They may have characteristics displaying efficiency, organisation, resourcefulness, and also show qualities of being very thorough in their play or perhaps the way they organise play.

Neuroticism (or emotional instability)

This is where your little one might encounter the world as a threatening and dark place. Your toddler might display feelings of anxiety, self-pity, feel tense and worry all the time, these are key personality traits for neuroticism.

These descriptions are called 'The Big Five' in the *The Developing Child*, by Denise Boyd and Helen Bee. [18] They provide a useful description of basic personality traits in toddlers, but these traits can move through to late childhood as well as adolescence, and surprisingly even adulthood.

Your little one may also display a few different traits not completely specific to one, which is of course completely normal. Despite the clear evidence that you are 'born with' a specific personality trait/temperament, environment may also strongly influence it.

The extent to which you as the parent direct your toddler's behaviour such as by showing warmth and in positively parenting them, can determine and change certain traits such as your little one being very shy, in showing her that it's okay and allowing her to take risks or express her personality more will allow your toddler to gain confidence in herself a little more also.

Emotional Intelligence

Most parents will take their 'job' as teachers seriously. They will teach their children colours, their ABCs, numbers, and how to brush their teeth properly. **but** we tend to neglect two important aspects of the lessons that we also need to be teaching: how to manage and name their feelings and how to understand other people's feelings.

The Gottman Institute define emotional intelligence as: "Emotional intelligence is about encompassing awareness, understanding, and the ability to express and manage one's emotions." [19]

In order to manage one's emotions they first need to be able to name it. Language development is a little like an iceberg, a great deal of the underlying emotion is underneath the surface.

According to Mary Sheedy Kurcinka, author of the book *Raising Your Spirited Child*:

> *"Two thirds of language development occur inside the brain, invisible to us. Months, sometimes years, before children are communicating with their own words, they understand those of other."* [20]

Parents who are learning to manage their toddler's intensity and **big** feelings might like to start by helping their child to name their emotions. For example:

You might start whilst soothing your crying baby saying to them softly that you understand that they are tired or maybe you might begin by saying to your toddler that you understand that they are feeling angry because it's time to come inside. Soon you will notice that your little one will start to use those words to express how they're feeling, they might say things like "I feel angry," or as my toddler likes to say "I have a hurt heart!"

So why does emotional intelligence really matter?

Deep down at our core we **all** know the answer to that!

You can't tackle a big project at work if you're riddled with anxiety. So how can we expect our children to tackle the play equipment or play nicely if they're also riddled with the stress of getting out the door so that you can be on time for your coffee/park date? You would also find it very difficult and confronting to work through your relationship issues without understanding and having some sort of perspective on how your partner and those around you emotionally work. So does your little one: they struggle with mistaking your stress and anxiety as *anger* at them.

Dr Laura Markham explains in her book *Peaceful Parent, Happy Kids*,[21] that a child's academic success will also be determined just as much as by their EQ (Emotional Quotient) as opposed to their IQ (Intelligence Quotient).

In my workshops and consultations parents have asked about school readiness and how to better prepare their children for that. The simple answer is that if they are emotionally in tune and their emotional wellbeing is relatively in check they will be school ready and able to learn because they won't be afraid to make mistakes. They will already be developing a growth mindset and they will be able to understand other children's feelings because they have an understanding of their own.

Did you know that your toddler is not actually born with emotional intelligence, that it is a learnt skill? Therefore, as parents you need the right tools to be able to teach your children about their feelings and how to better express themselves and how they feel in age appropriate ways.

This is the very essence of self-regulation, and a beautiful way for them to continuously find a way back to who they are.

Young children have not yet developed these skills at least not at the same level as us as adults. This difference in emotion regulation ability is the cause of **so** much stress for parents who have the expectation that their toddler has the same capabilities that they do, when in fact self-regulation takes years to develop.

Again, parents need to be working on brain integration, to make a well functioning whole. Just like a well functioning body, when your toddler's brain is not working well as a whole they will become easily overwhelmed by their emotions, confused and a little chaotic. As parents you want to help them to better use both sides of their brain so that they can think clearer and be a little more rational.

As parents you can assist brain integration by tapping into their emotional development. You can do this by simply speaking to your toddler about their feelings.

Let's be honest, when we are upset as adults the first thing that we want from our family and friends, our partner, is for them to hear us, lovingly and attentively, because their attention makes us feel understood and respected, we are usually more open to advice too.

Too often though as adults we try to halt our children's feelings. Perhaps we are upset or worried about what other people around us will think. Why?

First, and I'm going to be frank here, unless they are empathising with the situation at hand, they have no business being there to judge it. Second, it's not their space being consumed with an outburst of huge emotions: it's yours. And thirdly, regulating our emotions as adults is a mature skill to develop and takes many years.

Therefore, it's up to you to ignore family and friend's judgment, kneel down to your child's level and be all there in that moment with them. Give them a hug. Connection is key; remember it triggers those feel good endorphins and oxytocin in both of you. Take them away from the stimulation, and situation.

Let me share something with you. I went clothes shopping one weekend when our daughters were much younger. I remember feeling completely frazzled, not only because clothes shopping with three children in tow can be stressful anyway, but the music was **so** loud, there were voices and people everywhere, and I just couldn't think straight.

Our middle daughter was five at the time and incredibly sensitive to sensory overload (as she's gotten older we've all developed more awareness around her big emotions and at times the instability that was happening more often, we sought out play therapy). I could tell she was on the verge of a complete breakdown, which would usually entail her lashing out at one of us if we said something 'wrong.' She would also lash out with words or her hands or feet.

To avoid this happening in the middle of a busy shopping centre I gave her the tags from the pants I'd just bought in the hope that it might be a necessary distraction.

It was something so simple yet so needed. She needed to *play with something* to take her focus off the surrounding noise and stimulation. Too often we are told to 'ignore' our children's distress especially as they get older because we are told to think that 'they should know better.' But how would you feel if your feelings were ignored?

Read your children's cues, listen to them and how they're feeling? Treat them with the respect that they also deserve. No matter their age, hug it out with them. Be **all** there. Ask your toddler questions such as: "Are you feeling angry?" or "Do you think you might be feeling like that because your sister is playing with your toys?" Open ended questions create connection and conversation but also a better understanding.

In fact, there's a strong theme in all the research I've read: emotions make us healthy:

"A strong sense of wellbeing means much more than feeling happy all the time, or being free of illness. It is a combination of physical, social

and emotional factors."

(From *Helping your child to have a strong sense of wellbeing*, Issue No 4, Victoria Dept of Education and Early Childhood Development.)

Being able to control your emotions is an important part of our wellbeing. For example, when your little one asks for a glass of milk and instead you offer water. At first, their tears will well up, a melt-down might ensue: "I wanted milk!" But as they develop their emotional wellbeing rather than having a tantrum, your child might begin to take a deep breath and accept the water.

As they grow into older toddlers from three years to five, they are learning to control their emotional response to disappointment and to express their emotions a little more appropriately. Let's be honest here though, we as adults take years and years and years to develop our own emotional regulation. I'm in my late thirties and still express my feelings in a **big** way such as venting to my husband. I'm elaborating on this because I think it's really important to understand that, yes, emotion regulation is essential but we will **always** experience light and dark emotions too.

It's important that we do, so that we are whole. No person is happy 24/7 and the same can be said for anger and sadness, therefore it's essential that we teach our children to embrace all of their feelings as well. Teach them that it's normal to feel sadness, anger and anxiety but also that we can breathe through the feelings and watch them drift away so that they don't feel so intense.

Here are a few ways in which you can practically teach your children ways in which they can more readily tune into their emotions.

Acknowledge your toddler's perspective, be sure to empathise It's important to understand that even if you can't actually 'do anything' about your child's upsets, you still need to show empathy. Just being understood will help him let go of their upset.

How does empathy encourage emotional intelligence? Your toddler will feel understood. With understanding you start to trigger their neural pathways and strengthen them each time he feels soothed, it is what he'll then use to soothe himself as he gets older. Your toddler will learn to develop empathy because they are experiencing it from you. For little ones, just knowing that there's a name for their feeling is an early tool in learning to manage the emotions that will at times, flood them.

Allowing them expression Little ones can't discern between their emotions and their 'selves.' When you can begin to accept your toddler's emotions, rather than denying or lessening them, you are teaching them that all feelings are valid and necessary.

Disapproving of her fear or anger won't stop her from having those **big** feelings, but it may force her to begin to repress them if you deny her feelings in the first place.

Unfortunately, repressed feelings don't just fade away, as feelings do that have been freely and unconditionally expressed. Feelings that are repressed get trapped and need to look for a way out. Because they aren't under your child's conscious control, they pop out in unexpected ways such as when your child hits her sister, or maybe begins to have nightmares.

"When strong feelings such as anger, fear and frustration surface and they are ignored they don't just disappear. They simmer under the surface sometimes for a lifetime AND those feelings are scary to a child that doesn't know how to name it. Bottled up feelings can

lead to a profound sense of loneliness, their narrative could be 'no one understands me/no one sees me,' or even bursts of hysteria think 'drama queen!' or perhaps a little boy you may think needs anger therapy for anger issues … kids whose words of fear and frustration are repeatedly silenced may grow up emotionally disconnected "I'm NOT angry!! Meanwhile he's totally unaware that the veins in his head are poking out! That's not all, unexpressed emotions can lead to headaches, colitis, depression even cancer!!" Dr Harvey Karp, *The Happiest Toddler on the Block* [22])

Instead, as your toddler's parents you need to be teaching your child that the full range of feelings is understandable and part of being human.

Why does this encourage emotional intelligence? When you accept your child's feelings it encourages them to accept their own emotions, which then allows them to begin to resolve their feelings and move on, this is the beginning of emotion regulation for your toddler.

Your acceptance of your little one's feelings teaches them that their **big** feelings aren't dangerous. They are nothing to feel shame about, in fact their feelings are a normal part of being human, and that they're manageable.

When we accept them completely, **big** feelings and all, your little one will learn that even the less pleasant parts of herself such as her **big** feelings of sadness and anger are all acceptable, which means that she is wholly okay, just the way that she is.

Listen Whether your child is one year or 10, he needs you to listen to his feelings. Once he feels genuinely heard and acknowledged only then can he properly express them, he'll then be able to let them go and get on with the rest of his day.

You will be amazed at how affectionate and cooperative he will be once he has had the chance to show you how he really feels. But to feel truly safe in letting those feelings come up and out, firstly he will need to know that you are fully present and listening.

Why does this encourage emotional intelligence? The nature of healthy human emotions is to have them move through us, sometimes overwhelm us, and then inevitably float away. When we fight them off or repress them, emotions will get stuck inside us rather than finding their way to a healthy form of expression.

Children are often scared of their **big** strong feelings especially when they are overwhelmed by them, so they will try to fight them off by crying, screaming, and stomping until they feel safe enough to begin to feel them.

Laura Markham, founder of *aha! parenting*, says: "Because emotions are stored in the body, tantrums are nature's way to help young children vent." [23]

When you can help your child to feel safe enough to genuinely feel and express their emotions, you not only heal their psyches, their nerves and bodies, you also help them trust in their own emotional process so that as they grow older they are then better equipped to handle their own emotions without tantrums or repression. The way in which you react to your child's expression of emotions will contribute greatly to their health and wellbeing.

Take for example, *crying*. When we have a good cry, we feel better (I know I do!) When we have a good vent, maybe even punch a pillow, research has suggested that it lowers our blood pressure and helps us to recover, forgive and move on.

A child whose feelings are lovingly validated and acknowledged during the toddler years will grow up emotionally intact. They will know how to ask friends for help, how to better support others, and they will know how to name their feelings and support others that need to do the same. Remember that *respect* is just as important as love.

Owning your *reactions* and *responding* instead

I know for me that when love is flowing between myself and my girls, when we are tuned into each other and respecting and hearing one another, my life as a mama is pure bliss I could seriously burst with happiness and feel like I'm nailing life. **But** every well-meaning, well 'behaved' and well-loved child goes a little nuts at times. I know mine do!

We all have those days where we feel at the brink of explosion. Your three year old has spilled their cereal, your baby needs to be held at that exact moment making it difficult to mop it up and hold your crying toddler. You can hear your coffee pot bubbling and possibly getting burnt on the stove top, but still you choose to be here, with them instead.

There's nothing quite like the demands of a busy household, then throw in juggling work and kids too and it is seriously a time bomb about to go off. And at times that's exactly what we do, we go off. We find our anger and rage a perfect way to let out the pent up depression, anxiety and the build up of tension that goes with the busyness of being so busy.

We are fed up, exhausted, completely touched out and emotionally spent. I know that when I am at my lowest ebb of emotional turmoil I tend to focus on the negative aspects of everything around me, unfortunately that includes my children and especially how shit my mothering is too!

Anger is a strong emotion. One that we all struggle to stay calm through, especially with our children and ourselves when we are already at our lowest. As parents we are constantly experiencing triggers and at times have no idea where they've even come from. Anger is propulsive, it grabs you. You need to be at a place where you are mindful of those strong feelings, so that you can stop and breathe.

A practice I use and strongly encourage is to stop and breathe through your anger before it grabs you and propels you toward rage and reaction. You will be much quicker and able to respond to your child rather than react. So, before you react think about how you want to be remembered in this moment.

Do you want your three-year-old to look back at this time in their life and think "woah, mum/dad absolutely raged at us," or would you prefer them to look back at this time and think "gees, I really pushed mum/dads buttons and yet they were always so calm. Sure, they'd get angry, but they were almost always able to pull themselves out of it pretty quickly." When you can consciously breathe through your strong emotions you can come to a calmer state more easily.

Another way to survive the ebb and flow of your anger is to attend to each negative thought with acknowledgment. We all have angry and negative thoughts whilst in that emotional state of being, the worst thing that we can do is to shove it back down only for that stored up energy to rear its ugly head later.

When you are able to acknowledge your angry thoughts at the time and just say something in your head along the lines of: "Hey, I know you're angry and you want to strangle someone, we all get that way at times," or maybe you might prefer to acknowledge your negative thoughts with a: "Hey anger it's you again," instead.

As Sarah Napthali, author of *Buddhism for Mothers*, says:

"Accepting the existence of feelings such as hatred, loneliness, confusion, anger, guilt and resentment, is the only way to transform them into more wholesome states. Acceptance of life's unpleasantness without fighting, fleeing or forcing it out of awareness. We are also able to remind ourselves that by fully experiencing our emotions, we deepen our understanding of others pain and joy too." [24]

By acknowledging your angry thoughts, and breathing through them too, can create the space for a more productive conversation that comes from an authentic mindset rather than a reactive one.

What about **your** 'reactions'? For example, yelling and/or smacking. Know that it is unnecessary to *react* and so much more empowering to *respond*. Responding may look like you getting down to your little one's level or hugging to then reconnect in response to your little one's behaviour, but this is in fact you *owning* your 'reaction.'

Another simple but effective way to *own* your reaction can be to get down to your child's level and apologise for the way that you reacted. This alone can be incredibly empowering for your child. *But* also empowering for you. This is ultimately about you taking responsibility for your own actions, *and*, in turn, you are also teaching your child to do the same.

When you are in a place of acknowledgement and ownership of your own reactions it allows for connection and hopefully a discussion to take place. Most importantly it *always* creates the space for your toddler to feel safe again, as well as an opportunity for positive role modelling. Your actions and body language as a parent, as an adult, create far more meaning than the 'lectures' and discussions that you will ever have.

While we are on the subject of acknowledging and owning how you react I want to ask: Are you a **yeller**? Let's be real, we **all** yell at some stage of our parenting journey, sometimes we don't even notice that we are doing it. Our voices start to rise and get louder the more frustrated we become. Within that moment though you can even justify your actions and reactions.

But you and I both know that your kids respond better if you don't yell at them. Yelling almost always escalates the situation. It will make a tantrum turn into a storm and — let's get real here — how can you expect your child to learn self-control when you yourself have very little control over your own emotions?

Here are a couple of tips to stop yelling in its tracks *but* firstly you need to make a commitment to yourself *and* to your family. By doing so you are allowing accountability on your new parenting journey.

Simple steps to start with include:

- **Stop** yourself mid-sentence if you need to, and as soon as you can feel the anger bubbling at the surface; feel and hear your voice rising **stop** ... **breathe** ... take three deep breaths in and out.
- If you must, take yourself away from the situation. Start by saying "Okay, mummy/daddy can feel themselves getting really mad. I've taken some deep breaths, but I also need to move away for five minutes. You're safe you're okay, so I will be back in a minute." Then go and splash some cold water on your face to help slow down your reaction.
- Remind yourself that it's **not** an emergency. Remind yourself that they are acting like a child because they **are** a child.
- As soon as you feel calmer go back, try again.

Be kind to yourself too. Remind yourself that your reaction, your yelling, is coming from a place of fear from your 'fight or flight' response but you're working on it.

By stopping and taking deep breaths and coming back with a response rather than a reaction you **are** coming back to conscious and gentle parenting and that is always coming from a place of love.

As parents your child will naturally turn to you in times of comfort. They look up to you to show them quite literally, the way. They need assistance in the regulation of their emotions and you are their role model. For my daughters I know that if I'm upset-they're upset. If I'm teary, suddenly so are they. But if I'm calm they're calm as well.

It's a **huge** responsibility and sometimes I will literally feel the weight of it on my shoulders and in my heart, no doubt you do too.

> *"But researchers have described that self-regulation and the ability to calm ourselves, can lead to a biological change in our body."* Mary Sheedy Kurcinka, *Raising Your Spirited Child* [20]

Therefore, to help your children understand and manage their own emotions you have to commit to developing your own self-regulation skills first:

- Have you noticed that with fire you will nearly always fight fire?
- When you are practicing softening your approach your child will noticeably soften too.
- It does take **a lot** of patience, a few tears (on my part too!) but with your actions and words changing to a softer approach can change your child's intense reactions too.

Keeping in mind that energy can and does shift everything. When I am having a rough morning I'll make sure to walk it out after school drop off, instead of dwelling on how shit my morning just was. I'll instead create a mental gratitude list in my head. I begin by thinking of all the things that I am grateful for even something as simple as the opportunity to walk. I instantly feel lighter. It shifts your perspective and it changes the energy within. This is important self-love and work. about keeping alive this little human that we have been blessed with.

৯10৶

Understanding brain development

A S PARENTS WE tend to be focused on our children's diets and learning their manners and ABCs, yet we forget that an essential aspect of tuning into your children is also about having a little more understanding about their brain and how it works.

I am no neuroscientist, but I have loved learning more about the brain and in doing so it has allowed me to also learn more about my daughters and how to better tune into them and their feelings and behaviour.

To quickly sum it up: your toddler's brain plays a huge role in determining who they are and what they do. It is also shaped significantly by the experiences we parents offer them. When we know a little more about the brain and how we can better integrate both the left and right side it can help to nurture a stronger more resilient little person.

Your toddler's brain has many different aspects to it but for now we will only focus on the left and right brain and how we can better integrate them together.

Let's begin with the **left** side. This organises their thoughts and sentences. It loves order, it is logical, literal and likes words. The **right** side of their brain helps them to experience their emotions and to read non-verbal cues. It loves images, memories and is also very intuitive.

Your toddler has a 'reptile' brain that allows them to act instinctively and make split second survival decisions and a 'mammal' brain that leads them towards connection and relationships.

At the toddler stage your child will be right brain dominant. They are yet to master words and logic and will drop everything to watch a ladybug crawl across a leaf. They don't care that they'll be late for swimming lessons. Logic doesn't exist for them yet, but as soon as the word 'why' creeps into their language, you can bet it's a sure sign that their left brain is beginning to kick in.

There are many parts that make the whole and the key to thriving is helping these parts work together. *Integrating* is simply linking these different aspects together to make them a whole.

An example of integration are our bodies — our organs need to work together to form a healthy, functioning body. Our brains are much the same, our brain will perform at its best when its different parts work well together.

So, what does all of this have to do with your toddler?

It's simple. When your toddler is experiencing **big** feelings, it is because their brain is not yet functioning as a whole. They become overwhelmed and at times a little chaotic. They can't respond to you calmly or rationally, so they experience a meltdown and even aggression as a result of a loss of integration. Their little brain is not functioning as a whole.

We want your toddler to use both sides of their brain

Did you know that in recent years scientists have discovered through the use of brain scanning that the brain is actually mouldable, which means that the brain can physically change throughout the course of our lives?

So, what will create these changes? Experiences!

What your toddler *experiences* will literally change their brains. When they undergo a particular experience their brain cells become active or maybe you've heard of the term 'fire up.'

> "Did you know that your toddlers brain has one hundred billion neurones, each with an average of ten thousand connections to other neurones, this means that with mental activity or certain experiences within their lives certain neurones will fire together therefore growing new connections between them, over time these connections from constant firing (repeating the same or similar experiences) will rewire their brain." The Whole-Brain Child, by Dr Daniel Siegal and Tina Payne Bryson [25]

This means that as humans we aren't set to think a certain way or be a certain way for the rest of our lives, we can change and rewire our brains to be happier and healthier throughout the course of our lives.

In this moment your toddler's brain is constantly being rewired with the experiences that you are providing. Sounds like a tonne of pressure, right?

Don't worry, the basic parts of your child's brain will develop the way nature intends it too with proper nutrition, sleep and stimulation, genes will also play a role too!

With the research and findings that I have come across, everything that happens to us, the books we read, the music we hear the type of discipline we receive and the emotions we feel will all profoundly affect our brains. As parents you have the capacity to provide experiences that will help develop resilient kids!

I want to be clear here in regards to the word 'experiences.' I in no way want to put more pressure on you as parents. This does not mean wearing yourself out by incorporating activity after activity, buying a tonne of books so that they can quickly learn their ABCs or enrolling them into preschool five days a week so that they might get 'smarter.' By experiences I mean, presence, and connection, it really is that simple!

Daniel Siegal uses an analogy about a child rowing a canoe where a child whose brain is integrated will row down the middle of chaos and rigidity, they will feel harmonious. Your toddler frequently rows from rigidity to chaos within seconds, therefore they are feeling unruly, chaotic, and on the brink of a meltdown.

When you can see this is happening you can choose to *respond* rather than *react*, and choose calm over chaos so that you can gently veer them back to the middle of the river in their canoe, gently guiding them back to a state of wellbeing. When you see your toddler in a state of chaos and rigidity this is an early clue that they are in need of integration.

Parents having an insight into their behaviour, such as in the canoe analogy, will perhaps create the space early to use this as an opportunity to gently guide them back quicker to a state of wellbeing.

It can be very difficult to not intuitively copy aspects of how you were raised as a child because it literally becomes ingrained within us, but what I would strongly recommend is that we take a long hard look at ourselves as uncomfortable and confronting as that can be. Look very closely at the way that you are either parenting now or at how you have thought you might do so. Take a step back, journal it, meditate on it, talk it through with your partner. Will a particular parenting style serve your children well into their future? How will they remember you?

Without the understanding of your own childhood history, it can quite often repeat itself.

Daniel Siegel and Mary Hartzell Med in their book *Parenting from the Inside Out* say:

> *"How you make sense of your childhood experiences has a profound effect on how you parent your own children. In understanding more about yourself in a deeper way it can help you to build a more effective and enjoyable relationship with your children."* [26]

We all have some part of our childhood that we need to make sense of. Whether it be about a sibling and how they treated you or vice versa, it may be about one of your parents and the ways in which they spoke down to you or maybe as mentioned before, you were smacked, physically abused or sexually abused. There may have been periods of isolation, the silent treatment for days at a time. Yes, a heavy topic, one that most of us (including myself) find confronting and don't always feel comfortable in talking about it.

You can't change what happened in your past, and it is certainly not your fault, but you can take responsibility now, you can create understanding. It is not about denying your past but embracing it in order to move forward in your parenting journey. I'm going to start, I'm going to open up, so that we can move forward together.

When I was four years old I was sexually assaulted by our neighbour in an awful way. As I grew older I would seek attention from boys in very unhealthy ways. At the tender age of 15 I found myself in an emotionally and sometimes physically abusive relationship. The connection I had at such a young and impressionable age started innocently enough but slowly grew into forms of emotional abuse, he would cut me deeply with words that would sting such as commenting on my weight or my hairy eyebrows. He would lie on the couch and expect me to 'serve' him, and I did. I felt insecure and frumpy. Then came the comments on what I was wearing or how I did my hair. He openly cheated on me and didn't deny it when I'd confront him. This 'boy' then started to push me and pinch me, he'd slap me and visibly grope other teenage girls in front of me.

I was 21 years old when he left me and I'm forever grateful that he did because I don't think I'd have had the strength to. That moment in time was the beginning of my world turning upside down again. I moved out of home and partook in a lot of drugs, partying and all night benders. I attracted a host of disrespectful men and then I was raped.

This was a huge wake up call for me and a huge turning point in my life. The beginning of a long and much needed healing journey.

I was 23 years old when I started to take control of my own healing. I brought up a lot of 'stuff' that my family wasn't emotionally prepared to deal with but, intuitively, there was no other way. My soul was being called to start sifting through what was there, what needed to be let out.

It was raw, and it was messy and it leapt out from the flames and dark recesses of my soul. I couldn't control how I needed my voice to be heard and it got loud for a very long time.

Hindsight and self-reflection are a beautiful thing. After having children of my own I knew then why it was so important for me to have spoken up about my past to my family. I also knew that my reasons for reflection as I got older and became a mum was so that I could shine a light on my own darkness in order to embrace it and move into the light again.

I believe that we are a reflection unto ourselves and so in order to move forward sometimes we need to 'look back,' to not only create the space to heal but also able to seek out and better understand those sides of ourselves that we no longer want to be or repeat into our future.

I know now though that I needed to do that for my own healing. It was okay for me to talk about my experiences, and to begin to own my story. How others would react to that was no longer my problem — their reaction is always going to be their responsibility. We are responsible for our own healing however we need to do that.

When I think about becoming more of a conscious parent, in order for me to embrace my feelings about my childhood and adolescence, I truly felt that I needed to deeply understand and be authentic with my past, and my experiences, because as my girls grew older there were certain situations that I didn't feel comfortable with, such as, our girls playing with neighbourhood kids. There was no rhyme or reason for me to not feel comfortable with them having a playdate next door except for the fact that I didn't know them very well.

Those decisions came up for me and I felt icky and not okay with it, but I didn't understand the 'why' behind those feelings either. When I continued to reflect upon my feelings about it, my past experience of sexual assault bubbled up for me, and I needed to look at it a bit deeper and talk and share. I felt compelled to write about it, as well as express how I felt so I that I could parent our daughters in a way that resonated with my soul.

Being honest and authentic in my understanding of my life has allowed me to do better understand and support our daughters. I needed to talk about my past in order to move forward into my future and not continuously get caught up within the depths of it all. At some stage we need to let go, so we can move forward, but moving forward with a deeper understanding of who you really are too.

For you an example of a past childhood episode may not be as dark as mine. In fact, it might be something you won't even think about because it's not recognised as something that could be understood any deeper. An example could be spilling a cup of water or your chosen beverage as an adult. This happens more often then not and especially when someone says "Don't spill your drink!" Inevitably it happens, every time! This could be because as a child it was ingrained in you that it was a terrible thing that could happen. Unintentionally your parent would make you feel bad about the spilled water, and now it happens unconsciously as an adult. You're always spilling something.

As a parent, it is inevitable that we will experience some triggers from our own childhood. As a parent yourself you might start coming from a place of 'reacting' rather than 'responding' to your own children. You might find yourself yelling at them for spilling that cup of water and upon reflection you'll know that that has come from your own childhood and it doesn't need to be something you'd like to repeat.

Next time they spill the glass of water, you will then respond by perhaps getting down to their level and saying something like "We've spoken about having our cups of water in the kitchen only. If I find it in the loungeroom again, we will have to go back to drinking only out of our drink bottles in the house again."

Another example of childhood wounds repeating themselves may come in the form of you being overprotective, or possibly withholding affection. Another example might be giving so much affection that it becomes claustrophobic for your children. You may even react with a strong emotional response such as a smack on the bottom or impulsive behaviour such as screaming.

These intense reactions can create feelings of animosity between you both. It is at these times that we are not acting like the parents we wish to be.

When we have more of an understanding about who we are and how we were raised, where those 'reactions' or ways of 'being' have come from, then there will be a deep sense of personal and spiritual growth. You will start to discover the very essence of what felt 'right' for you when you were a child, and what didn't. And what you'd like to take with you on your unique parenting journey and what you wish to leave behind.

This self-realisation will change your relationship into a deeper, more enriched connection because you are creating a different found-ation. One that you wanted as a child and are now able to gift to your own children.

As Daniel Siegel and Mary Hartzell Med say in their book:

"Research has shown that without such self-understanding history will continue to repeat itself as negative patterns are passed down throughout the generations to come" [26]

When we become parents, we are blessed with the most incredible gift, the gift of being able to grow into the kind of parents we see ourselves as being, an opportunity to raise our children consciously, the next generation of human beings. How do you wish that future generation to be? Empathetic? Generous? Kind? Big hearted? By being and modelling those qualities, we will teach them that!!

Our children are sponges, they trap, hold and swell with everything said to them and absorb all that surrounds them. Try to be mindful of the words that you choose to use. As parents, we have chosen to use words and actions that will empower our sons and daughters, that will show them compassion for all creatures and human beings, and at all times we try to demonstrate as best we can, empathy, kindness, as well as love, **always**.

When we live from a conscious heart and head space we *choose* daily, no matter how exhausted we are, to live from that thoughtful and conscious space as much as we humanly can. We won't get it 'right' all of the time, because there is no perfect way of parenting, but we can do the best that we can with the knowledge and inner knowing that we already have within!

The transformation into parenthood blesses us with **the** most incredible opportunity to grow as individuals. The communication patterns that we set up now and nurture with ourselves and our children will help to create secure and trusting relationships in all aspects of their lives now and into the future.

Parenting is not about who is right or who is wrong. Instead, let's shift our thinking to parenting as an almost endless opportunity to learn about how to shift our own thinking and behaviour to bring about change within our own unique view of the world that we live in. Reflection on how we are parenting allows for that self-growth to happen, it will also allow for self-growth within ourselves as human beings.

When we begin to lean into an empathetic understanding for our own parents, and our past, when we choose to lead with compassion and kindness in our own parenting journey, we can then begin to apply this into our everyday lives with our own families as well as those around us, thus creating more peaceful homes, extending into fostering peaceful relationships and friendships and ultimately creating a more peaceful World.

An understanding of who I am has always been a strong driving influence for me as I hope it is for you too, as parents we will always influence our children in some way.

Becoming a more conscious parent is an act of self-reflection for you both. When you are able to facilitate an open hearted discussion on how you would like to move forward as a family, when you are willing to discuss the light and dark shades of your past childhood wounds and learnings, as well as discuss what aspects of both your childhoods you resonate with and would like to bring forth into your parenting journey, this then becomes the first step in parenting on the same page as well!

Parenting from a mindful and conscious perspective starts with communication. How do you want your children to feel when you talk to them? Will your conversation begin with words such as "Here comes my little dude," or will it be "Oh no, here comes trouble." As parents we make an impact in their world with the words and, more importantly, the actions that we choose to use daily.

We are choosing to either characterise and connect with them in a positive way or we risk demoralising their sense of self and slowly but surely begins the disconnect.

Why? Because the interactions with you are negative and it doesn't feel good for them. If we don't begin to think consciously about the words that we choose to use to characterise our children's behaviour, then how we speak to our children and who we think we are raising is who they will become.

So, yes, perhaps you were spoken to negatively in your own childhood. As I've mentioned, childhood wounds tend to creep up without us even realising it. Without some understanding and acknowledgment about your own history, it will quite often repeat itself. According to Siegel and Med:

"How you make sense of your childhood experiences has a profound effect on how you parent your own children. In understanding more about yourself in a deeper way it can help you to build a more effective and enjoyable relationship with your children."

When we make the decision to parent from this conscious perspective, together, we also need to take into account the process of patience and time so that you as parents can lean into learning about each other's varied needs. I have mentioned this previously also, but I feel it's important to repeat in the context of choosing your words wisely.

When we begin our parenting journey we do so with hugely vast expectations which is fine because we weren't brought up the same way or with the same parents. It, therefore, is so important to discuss the values you wish to impart as well as the ways in which you wish to raise your little people preferably before your baby is here, but if not afterwards.

When we lead together and parent consciously we do so with respect. Neither of you will know each other's true experience of childhood but what you can do is listen, value each others truth and story and lean into the vulnerability of it all and the bravery in sharing. When we do this we truly get to a place of trust and empathy.

When we do this we really lean into each other as a whole, there is no room for judgement only love and acceptance. This will enable you to both get down to the grit of each others values systems and the real depth of how you wish to raise your children.

Together, you are evolving and learning as a new family laying down the building blocks that will unavoidably take you all on a journey of discovery.

❧ 11 ❧

Reclaiming the spark within

WE ARE CRANKY, they get cranky.

We stare at our screens because it's the path with less conflict and struggle.

We're busy, they're **too** busy!

We punish rather then choose to teach.

We forget to stop. Listen and connect.

Sometimes it's all too much. It's too trying, too tiring and too damn challenging.

There are days where it feels like it is **so** okay to be a grump.

We've woken up to another sleepless night and all of our children are still in the bed.

You've had to scrub texta marks off the wall all because you had an extra 10 minutes lie in.

Milk has been spilled all over your brand-new rug, it was in your favourite mug too and now that's in pieces on the floor!

Parenting can be hard. It can be stressful. The question is, is it worth deliberating and dwelling upon things that you cannot change? Things that have already happened. Isn't that a recipe for making you feel worse?

Dr Justin Coulson has researched over 1000 Australian parents, and says in his book *10 Things Every Parent Needs to Know* [27] that they experience lowered wellbeing as their children have gotten older or with the more children that they have had: "Research has shown that children create unhappiness. There are some parenting blogs and *Facebook* feeds that actually perpetuate that."

Dr Coulson goes onto explain that he found children are more likely to think that they are the cause of their parent's frustration, anger and sadness. Could it be because we show our negative feelings far more than we do our joy, or our happiness?

There is no doubt that parenting challenges us, it can take us to a dark place that we didn't even know existed. But does this mean that in being a parent we can no longer find the 'joy?'

Let's look at the word 'meaning,' which itself means 'something meant or intended.'

Taking the existence of your child as an example, *meaning* means to look at what you have achieved with your parenting journey: the giving, the selflessness, the sacrifice and love, all of this experience brings joy, and a sense of purpose in your parenting journey. There are numerous experiences that we can have with our child/ren to feel more joy and more happiness in our everyday together.

Connection

When we connect and listen, we show our children that their feelings are important. Connection is always key to leading with love and warmth. It takes work but the outcome is always magical. When we create time for meaningful connection with our kids every day, reconnection takes place and it makes them feel loved. It's not to say that without the connection you're not loving them **but** with connection they actually genuinely **feel** it.

For you as the parent, reconnecting with your children creates opportunities for you to get to know them better. It also helps you slowdown from your 'stuff.' And we **all** need that.

Simple ways that you can connect can be looking for opportunities to talk, such as in the car on the way home from preschool/school. Ask questions that are open, such as "what was the funniest thing you learnt at school today?" Or "Who did you play with and what games did you play?" This shows interest in their everyday.

You can read together on the couch. Put down your phone, show them that you care and want to connect, look at them when they are excitedly sharing their day. Show them that they are important to you, because even on your busiest day you can still find the time to **stop** and **connect**.

Hug

Hugging creates a burst of the 'love' drug oxytocin. Big hugs also give you a burst of dopamine and serotonin. These are all-natural brain chemicals that create bonding and promote a positive sense of being. So, hug, hug and always hug!

Spending time in nature

Biophilia, is defined in the dictionary as: "An innate love for the natural world, supposed to be felt universally by humankind." Time in nature creates a sense of peace and connection. Unhurried time and gratitude for all that surrounds us. Often our daily and somewhat trivial dramas can disappear once we set foot onto the soft warm sand or feel the green grass between our toes.

Foster an attitude of Gratitude

If we can appreciate the simple things in our lives such as drinking our coffee while its still hot or having an opportunity to sleep in uninterrupted, our sense of wellbeing and joy is increased. Today, think of two simple things that you are grateful for, or better yet, write it down. Hold onto that feeling and sense of peace for the rest of your day.

To take your practice of gratitude deeper, start a gratitude journal (as previously mentioned) and every day make space to write a list of the things that you are grateful for. Start small then add onto it daily.

Slow down

Why are we always having to be somewhere, or do something? I challenge you to have a whole day at home pottering around, playing with your children reading a book or the paper. No screen time put all devices on aeroplane mode and see how you feel after one whole day of doing very little. Savour the little things. Relish in the simplicity and find your joy as a parent!

Dating your partner

Parenting is consuming. There are long nights and even longer days, very little time in between for you to fit in what you would like to do let alone factor in time with your partner. This is important. If there is no time for you as a couple, then the spark that initially started your beautiful family will fall away.

For us, we didn't have family that we could rely heavily upon whenever we found an hour or two up our sleeve, or blessedly was able to either pump a few millilitres of milk, or our baby had spread their feeds out to a three hour gap, so hallelujah! let's lock in a date night. **but** we didn't have parents that could drop things with a few hours' notice. So, we created date nights at home.

The thing is we over complicate date nights. We think we need to get all dressed up, book a table at our favourite restaurant (which after all this time probably isn't our favourite restaurant any more) share a bottle of wine, maybe go for a long beach walk afterwards, or hit the dance floor or maybe we feel that we need to go home and make love a few times for old times' sake!

In reality, we have just made another list of 'things to do' when it should just flow organically at this point. It is really just about spending a little time together and creating space for that to happen without the television on, phones off and no computers!

Ours became a Friday night ritual, something to look forward to at the end of a long week. We would put our little ones to sleep (you see we didn't catch onto the whole 'date night' thing until we were well into being parents of two children. I'm giving you this advice early I hope!). My hubby would make us a pizza and we would share a bottle of wine and talk. It was exactly what we needed!

So we made it a weekly ritual. We didn't need to find a babysitter because it was completely no fuss and we still were able to reconnect amongst the sleep deprivation. It undoubtedly saved us.

Date nights don't even have to be just the two of you it can be in the form of a 'family date night.' As our kids have grown, we have also evolved into Friday nights being a family movie night, possibly after a great day at the beach, and then come home salty and tired. We'll set ourselves up in the lounge room and watch a movie with some wine and yummy food.

Your date night might look different to ours. It might be that you have a supportive family which can babysit your little one with short notice, so you can dress up and hit the town. Do it! Whatever works for you, whatever makes your soul sing, whatever allows you the space to reconnect go and do that, you will not ever regret spending more time together alone once your little love is earth-side. After all, you are their foundation.

∽ 12 ∽

Reconnected parenting

S O HOW DO WE find our *flow* in surrender? As parents we all have far too much to do.

Our modern lives are focused around productivity, both at work and in our home, most days I feel a constant need, both internally and externally, to have 'done something' with my day, to be ticking items off my long to-do list. But what if what we really need, every now and then, is just to do nothing?

To hibernate, to disconnect from the outside world a little more (and more importantly the online world) and opt for a deeper connection with our loved ones. What would it feel like to entrench ourselves in our emotional and spiritual wellbeing? Perhaps we could begin with putting down our phones and actually checking in with each other.

There is a distinct sense of mindfulness when we are truly in the moment with our children and our families. There will be plenty of time to move forward personally whether it be within your career or personal life, but how much time is there really for a mindful connection with your children while they're still young and seeking time that is spent with you?!

There will be many opportunities as your children grow up for them to explore and get outside of their comfort zones. To fill up your days until your cups our overflowing and to complete your to-do lists with exclamation marks.

But equally, there is always a time and a season for *hibernation*, to really choose to slow down and set your mind towards soothing your family's soul with a genuine and mindful connection. To others, it may appear that you're doing nothing. That you're wasting your precious time. Saying "no" to a catch up and opting out of endless playdates and activities. In fact, what you are doing is saying "yes" to creating some much-needed space.

As parents we are always putting an imprint of love and connection into our children's hearts and minds when we consciously choose to slow down. Unknowingly, we are creating space to talk, to laugh, to play and to just to be.

We live in a fast-paced world and life can seem more then a little overwhelming at times. By the time we are parents we are already so used to being busy. We tend to be goal driven, career minded and all about 'self' as we start out on our parenting journey. We have already lost the capacity to deeply relax, and we rarely say "no."

When we are able to access that part of ourselves again that can 'switch off,' we are also teaching our children too that it's okay to slow down. That it's okay to be mindful of quiet time and reconnection. That it's okay to be bored and to not have to be 'doing' things all the time.

I feel so much that the greatest opportunity of this time in our lives is within our four walls of our own homes. Not only are we in an era of *busy* being seen as commendable but we are also within a new period of sharing our lives online, however beautiful it seems. It can also have us feeling like we're so significant, with so much to prove and to be, or in fact feel really insignificant for the same reasons.

We identify so much with what's on our 'insta' bio or in the other public squares we share. We identify ourselves with what we share online when it is really just our 'highlight reel?' Isn't our 'real life' waiting for us outside of our screens? Is it just 'modern times, get used to it'? Or can we begin to start paying a little more attention? I worry that we are giving this so much of our own energy both as parents and as humans living in this modern age. There must be so much more beyond our own homes and families while our children are still so young.

I know that many of us have work to do outside of our homes, but can we use certain seasons (perhaps the colder months) as an chance to say 'no' to the outings and social events and use the time productively to potter around at home with our little ones? To get back to playing, reading together and 'being' within each other's company?

For me, there has always been a real sense of beauty in surrender, in going with the flow and forsaking the need to constantly get yet another thing done on my 'to do list.' In our home we tend to use the cooler months to hibernate, to slow down and nourish ourselves. In particular for me, my spiritual self, to reconnect with our girls, play board games and colour-in, to read books, and paint our nails.

Maybe use this time to create much needed space for your partner to reconnect and talk over a bottle of wine, watch *Netflix* and enjoy each other's company. As the cooler weather surrounds us, give your family permission to find the joy in 'missing out,' to restore your family's inner peace and to create a deeper, enriched and mindful reconnection again

Seeking self compassion

Guilt

Some mamas say they never live a day without it. We worry. Did we give enough of our time today? Did I feed him well enough? She hardly slept today and yesterday. Is she cutting her day sleeps or was it because I met my girlfriend for a coffee?

We feel overstretched by the demands of a busy household, the juggle of work and our kids. Spending time with friends and your partner. There are days where we might think to ourselves 'is this it? Is this part of some divine plan to have me feeling like a nervous wreck!?'

Motherhood introduces us to so many varied mind states, such extremes of emotions that can feel so unfamiliar and at times disturbing. We will swing from one to the other. Revisiting old wounds, and hurts.

We also try to hide all of these feelings due to undulating pressure on ourselves and from our friends and family, society as a whole because we are supposed to feel 'good' about being in this place called mamahood. We are so quick to judge each other too for feeling all of this and some. Then those mama guilt feelings come up again because we shouldn't be feeling this way. Most harshly though, we will judge ourselves.

Anxiety can creep in ever so slowly, along with feelings of despair and loneliness, boredom and restlessness. All of this, along with feelings of more guilt for feeling this way and feeling anything but 'blessed.'

As a parent there are so many 'should do's,' 'I should be more patient.' I should be more organised.' Often this word tends to activate the disobey button in us & we do exactly what we 'should not!' For example, drinking a glass of wine on a Monday night when we have said to ourselves 'Ah, I really shouldn't!'

When we are tired from all of the 'should do's' that we 'should' be doing, we tend to take it out on our little ones, and we will snap. Instead of thinking to yourself, 'I really 'should' have more patience' perhaps it would be a better alternative to look at the 'why' for your reaction.

What's coming up for you to allow your never ending *to do* list to create stress and disharmony, thereby taking it out on your child/ren because you lack energy? Is this an opportunity for you to take that 10 minutes out for yourself and **stop** the mama guilt and the 'I should be doing this list?'

Because in the end, who is that really benefitting? Yes, your laundry's done, your dishes are clean, your house is tidy, dinners cooked, and the cars been washed, but could at least one of those 'should do's' be completed later or even tomorrow? Could you have taken that opportunity for *you* and then felt better for doing that therefore more able to connect with your little people rather than get short with them?

"Parents aren't perfect people. They're people being perfected." (LR Knost)

We need to start dropping our expectations on ourselves and open ourselves up as non-judgementally as possible to whatever is happening for us at the time.

Because in those moments of sacrifice, when we are always putting our children's needs before our own, in those sleepless nights and the 'trying to keep calm' throughout a long tumultuous tantrum, when the housework is piling up, the never-ending list of your 'should do's' has begun, it is in such moments that we need to be kind to ourselves.

We need to show ourselves some self-compassion because we are doing it, and we are amazing!

This brings me to *Self-Compassion*. We have already discussed the
fact that we all will likely experience some form of parental guilt on the
daily.

You may notice as a parent that you're feeling angst and guilt
about the same things day in and day out. Could it be that feeling
guilty and letting that 'feeling' in isn't working for you? Guilt creates so
much frustration and self-loathing it is a repetitive attack upon yourself as a human being, not just as a parent.

To practice self-compassion is to ultimately encounter oneself, to
look at you and see your own unique daily struggles. Know that they
are okay. Take responsibility for your 'reactions' know that it is normal
to 'react' to your child/ren rather then to 'respond' sometimes; apologise for your 'reaction,' and try not to take it too personally.

This will allow for a discussion to take place, and it will *always*
create the space for renewed connection, as well as an opportunity for
positive role modelling. Again, your actions and words as a parent, as
an adult, create far more meaning than the 'lectures' and discussions
that you will ever have.

We *all* feel somewhat guilty for how we have reacted to a situation with our toddler but by staying stuck in your guilt is like saying
"I am all mighty and powerful I make everything turn to shit alllll by
myself!" Therefore, this mistake, this action, this shitty thing that you
have done, is just a small part of your story.

It doesn't define you. Your mistakes are not the definition of who
you are as a person. As a parent. Forgive yourself and let it go.

As a mum, no matter where you are on your parenting journey,
the new reality with our precious child/ren can make us feel like we

are 'losing' ourselves. In fact, it is the complete opposite, being a parent gives us the opportunity to find more of ourselves. It can give us a chance to seek out the depth of who we are or who we were, so that we can reach that aspect of ourselves and become **more** of who we are, more of what we want to become today.

This is the understanding that your child has come to teach you and allow you to grow as a human being. Parenting will bring you to the core of your ego, always. Our children trigger us because they are ours: "I will be the best parent", "I will be the best mother." As author Dr Shefali Tsabary says in her book *The Conscious Parent*: "Every time we fall short of these expectations our children trigger us, but what our children are really doing is showing us a mirror to our underdeveloped self." [28]

Let's get real, we are a slave to time, we live with an obsession of 'getting stuff done,' we are always building something, learning something, achieving something. When we slip into this notion of thinking it is too easy for us to pull our children into our own arrangements, our own 'stuff' and becoming more and more insensitive to their unique needs. We don't enjoy being parents because our minds our elsewhere. Hello mama guilt!

When we do focus on present parenting though, our minds and our hearts will shift dramatically, straight into the core of that moment. You're there and you're free from all of the worry, all of the 'should do's.' We do live within an age where busyness is becoming a virtue and, because of this, it can create the very same expectations in our children.

We are giving our children the message that *hyperdrive* is a normal state of mind. If we're not doing all of the 'should do's' then we are feeling guilty about it. This will eventually create a serious disconnect because we do not possess the capacity to slow down.

We then run the risk of creating this for our own children, who will blossom into teenagers and then young adults, but who do not understand the meaning of balance and in slowing down because they haven't seen what that looks like, we haven't shown them. There is no doubt that with multiple children, work and a home to run, that we all can sit in overwhelm and cannot possibly avoid 'busyness.' But we can still be present within those busy times.

❧ 13 ❧

Present parenting through mindful living

PARENTING MINDFULLY is huge for me as a mother of three young daughters. It's so easy to get caught up in life, in its everyday distractions, rushing around with a mind full of stress and thinking about the future. By being aware of our present moments it teaches us to become more aware of the time spent with our children.

"Mindfulness is an awareness of the present moment, the sensations & feelings that may arise, by being able to observe our emotions we can ensure a life more fulfilled" (Sarah Napthali in *Buddhism for Mothers*[24])

For me it is about learning from my mistakes. For example, I had a difficult time getting out the door in time for school to start. I was snapping and irritable at my children because they were not listening. When we finally got into the car, I had a simple choice: I can choose to stay in that negative mindset, or I can choose to move through it. I chose to move through it and to look a little deeper. What buttons did my girls push? And why? What is really happening for my girls in that moment? And how could I reconnect with them?

Turns out once I slowed down to reconnect with my eldest daughter in particular, her behaviour ran far deeper then what was 'annoying' her and myself in that negative moment past, she was anxious about a maths test at school that day so she was reacting to everything I said out of fear and bottled up anxiety. If I hadn't taken that deep breath, if I hadn't stopped to genuinely reconnect with her, I would have missed that crucial moment to find out what was **really** going on, not only that but an opportunity to show her that I do have the time for her, to really hear what's happening for her.

Again, Sarah Napthali in *Buddhism for Mothers*:

"With mindfulness we are more aware of who are children are and we are more able to free them from any pressures to fulfil unrealistic expectations."[24]

Practising mindfulness brings a sense of wisdom because only with mindfulness within the present moment in front of us, do we have any hope of understanding 'what is.' What really is happening right now, not what you are perceiving it to be, what you are 'thinking' is happening, the 'story' that you are telling yourself.

How mindful are you really? To what extent are you missing when it comes to being present with your children?

Let me share another story with you. As a child, and even now, my parents have always been a little scatty. I mean this in a way of *presence*. There was always something else on or happening around them and rarely time for real presence. Even now, when I call, it's difficult to get a true moment alone where there is real connection and attention.

I cannot deny that feeling of sadness that creeps up sometimes during a phone call or catch up, that feeling of not always being completely understood.

I made a promise to myself early on as a new mum that I would try to be as present as I could be when my children were talking to me. This is not just because of the way I myself have felt in the past (and even now) but also because I truly believe that right now, in that moment, it is important to show your children that they matter just by simply listening and giving them your complete attention when they are talking to you. This shows them that you do care about their 'little things' the things that inevitably build trust and which are essential for when they are older. Hopefully, your child will then feel comfortable being able to share their 'big things' with you.

Being aware of the present moments around us teaches us more about ourselves and it also enables connection and quality time with our children. It is a time of learning and personal growth.

Another important aspect of being mindful is *acceptance*, defined by the dictionary as the act of *accepting* something or someone.'

What is *acceptance* for you? For me it is about accepting the winds of change. Not over-analysing them. It is the *inner knowing* that just as the seasons change, so do we, as human beings and as parents.

Full disclosure: I struggle greatly with change. I always feel flat days before our children grow a year older. I don't always know what 'moving forward' means for me on a personal or professional level and that sometimes scares me. I struggle with the cooler seasons and the change that brings. But change is inevitable.

Could it be that if we are more mindful of the moments happening in front of us, when we are truly present, we will no longer be thinking about the changes that are happening around us?

I've come to realise, however, with time and becoming more mindful, that change is nothing to be feared because change equals growth. Probably a scary thought to many. We are present and mindful within our daily moments, then change happens without another thought. It just happens. When dinner's not on the stove and if your children aren't in the shower by five pm, what will actually happen if those activities don't happen at that time?

Nothing. Because you are being present, you are flowing and moving through the ebbs of life with children, therefore you are no longer thinking about the change that will inevitably happen, such as a possible later bedtime, and you are calmer. You are ok with the imperfection of what is, after all, just being in the *now*.

Every day when we wake up, we can *choose* to accept the day as It will be, **or** we can fight it. With acceptance comes a calmer sense of self which in turn creates a calmer home life too.

Being mindful of the stresses around you and in your life can bring about a sense of self awareness. Do stop. Do take notice. What are the thoughts running through your mind? How is stress affecting your body? How does it feel?

Be mindful

When we are being mindful as parents, as humans, when we are choosing to be in that present moment with ourselves, is when we are being our authentic self. This is when we are not comparing ourselves to others, we are not distracted, we are all there, in that moment.

If we can practice this more often, practice it only once daily. We will judge ourselves less (I really should not be reading this magazine I need to put washing on, oh shit, I am such a terrible housewife.) We will live more authentically (because we are being ourselves rather than comparing ourselves to others, aka social media.) And we are living right here in the present, there is no future, and no past, just there in that exact moment.

How we choose to live our own lives can sometimes be our best teachers. Be gentle with yourself. We are **all** learning and you are doing the work when you create the understanding that you want to 'break the cycle' that you're in. So, be kind to you, because you are doing the best that you can. In the end we all are.

Present parenting is about coming from a place of deep connection. When being in the present moment with your child, when listening and connecting, tune into them with your whole self, turn away from the distractions and the noise: 'listen and be present.'

Silence yourself and try not to think about what to say next or how to 'fix' their 'problem.' The 'problem' might not need to be fixed. Maybe all your child needs is a sounding board, someone to talk to and someone that will listen to them with their whole heart.

Mindful living especially as a parent comes down to the way we use our words as well as the tone and our body language. All of this demonstrates our way of being with our children.

Shefali Tsabary perfectly describes some ways in which you can inspire your child to live their best life:

"to help your child realize the abundance of which they already exude, you can tell them such things as 'you inspire me,' 'I am in awe of who you are,' 'I am amazed by your spirit,' 'you take my breath away,' 'your capacity for kindness is huge,' 'you are a true person,' 'your ability to imagine and create is extraordinary,' 'you are blessed with so many talents,' 'you are rich within,' 'you have so much to teach me,' 'I learn how to be a better person from you." [28]

Remember that children learn by what is said and in how they live.

Mindful parenting is an essential part of being a conscious parent, and it is a lifelong practice. It is about becoming less attached to the outcome and more mindful of what is unfolding in yours and your children's lives.

The most important part of spiritual growth on our journey into *be-coming* a mother is our self growth, our capacity to self reflect and process what our triggers are and why they come up for us, what isn't serving us or who and when the time to 'let go' might be.

Parenting consciously is a way that we can all parent if we are open to further growth and a deeper learning about ourselves so that we can grow and learn together along with our children, our greatest teachers.

About the author

NIKKI SMITH is a registered nurse and maternal child and family nurse and is currently studying counselling. She is the founder and Director of **Earthway Parenting** (www.EarthwayParenting.com.au) and has contributed to numerous publications such as *The Natural Parent Magazine*, *Green Child Magazine* and *The Holistic Parenting Magazine*.

Nikki is passionate about supporting, nourishing and guiding families to feel more self empowered in raising their children from birth into early childhood, with attachment, connection and awareness. She believes that if we can support our children in a more wholistic, aware and gentle way then we can begin to parent with more compassionate understanding. In doing so we will raise more confident, emotionally mature, loving and trusting children.

With her husband and three daughters, Nikki lives on the Central Coast of NSW, Australia where she facilitates workshops both online and in person, as well as one-on-one consultations focusing on gentle parenting approaches to support and guide families.

Recommended further reading

Infant care and connection

- Jean Liedloff: *The Continuum Concept*
- Sarah Napthali: *Buddhism for Mothers*
- Attachment parenting Australia: http://www.attachmentparentingaustralia.com/index.htm
- Elizabeth Pantley: *The No Cry Sleep Solution*
- Ina May Gaskin: *Ina May's Guide to Childbirth* and *Spiritual Midwifery* (both books cover post-partum)
- Heng Ou: T*he First Forty Days*
- Dr Oscar Serrallach: *Postnatal Depletion Cure*
- Dr Harvey Karp: *The Happiest Baby on the Block*

Toddler years

- Dr Harvey Karp: *The Happiest Toddler on the Block*
- Jan Hunt: *The Natural Child: Parenting from the Heart*

- LR Knost: *Whispers Through Time*
- Sarah Naphali: *Buddhism for Mothers of Young Children*
- Patty Wipfler & Tosha Schore: *Listen*
- Mary Sheedy Kurcinka: *Raising your Sprited Child*
- Dr Bob Jacobs: *Perfect Parents, Perfect Children*
- John Gottman & Joan DeClaire: *Raising an Emotionally Intelligent Child*
- Dr Daniel Siegal: *No Drama Discipline*

Brain development

- Dr Daniel Siegal: *The Whole Brain Child*

Reparenting

- Dr Daniel Siegal & Mary Hartzell: *Parenting from the Inside Out*
- Bessel Van Der Kolk: *The Body Keeps the Score*
- Alice Miller: *The Drama of the Gifted Child*
- Dr Nicole LePers: *How To Do The Work*

Motherhood

- Karen Maezen Miller: *Mama Zen*
- Amy Taylor Kabbaz: *Mama Rising*

Mothering daughters

- SuEllen Hamkins & Renee Schultz: *The Mother–Daughter Project*
- Dr Christiane Northrup: *Mother–Daughter Wisdom*
- Steve Biddulph: *Raising Girls*
- Kasey Edwards & Dr Christopher Scanlan: *Raising Girls Who Like Themselves*

Mothering sons

- Steve Biddulph: *Raising Boys*
- Maggie Dent: *Mothering our Boys*
- Maggie Dent: *From Boys to Men*

Acknowledgements

I am indebted to my husband Ben, because without his push, guidance, unwavering support and love, as well as providing copious cups of tea and wine (!) I don't think I'd have had the gusto to have finished this book when I did.

A sincere thank you to Andrew from Radiate Publishing who edited my manuscript and supported me in continuing the publishing journey so that I could get this book into the hands of as many parents as possible. Your time and generosity has meant the world to me.

Beth, you were always a supportive friend and mentor and were there with me from the very beginning when this book was literally only a seed, a thought, and an idea. You believed in me and pushed me to start writing. You inspired me to follow my dreams and I will forever be thankful for you, your kindness, your intellect, and your inner beauty, always.

A **huge** thank you to **all** my beautiful friends and family who have supported me on this book writing journey; you know who you are and I love you so!!

Lastly, but the most important thank you is for **all** the beautiful, open hearted parents who have ever attended one of my workshops or consultations, you are the inspiration behind this book -- it was always written for you.

And to you the reader, thank you for opening yourself up to the writings and discoveries within this book. I truly hope it will guide you throughout those early years and be a book you can always come back to within those difficult times of sleep deprivation, guilty parenting, and meltdowns!

My hope has always been for this book to be a resource that can lift you up when times are hard, to be an honest guide and reflection into modern day parenting as well as a tool to open up discussions around your childhood and to enable growth from there as both a parent but also as a human being.

Parenting is a journey, it's not a destination, so stay open and curious. Be the love and calm that you want your children to see in the World because positive change within the four walls of our homes becomes the change that happens all around us

References

1   Saru M Matambanadzo's, *The Fourth Trimester*, <https:// repository.law.umich.edu/mjlr/vol48/iss1/3/>.

2   Ina May Gaskin, *Spiritual Midwifery*, Book Publishing Company, 4th edn, 2002.

3   Royal Women's Hospital, Melbourne, *The Baby Blues*, <https://www.thewomens.org.au/health-information/preg nancy-and-birth/mental-health-pregnancy/baby-blues>.

4   Susan Krauss Whitbourne, 'The 4 Principle of Attachment Parenting,' *Psychology Today*, <https://www.psychologytoday. com/au/blog/fulfillment-any-age/201307/the-4-principles- attachment-parenting-and-why-they-work>.

5   Jan Hunt, *The natural child, parenting from the heart*, New Society, 2001.

6   Diane Benoit, 'Infant-parent attachment: Definition, types, antecedents, measurement and outcome,' *The Paediatric*

Child Health Medical Journal, <https://www.ncbi.nlm.nih. gov/pmc/articles/PMC2724160>.

7   Bob Jacobs, *Perfect Parents Perfect Children: Changing the World by Celebrating our Perfection*, Ocean Reeve Publishing, 2020.

8   Jean Liedloff, *The Continuum Concept*, Little Brown, 1986

9   Red Nose Organisation (UK), *Sharing Sleep Surfaces with Baby*, <https://rednose.org.au/downloads/InfoStatement_SharingSleepSurfacewithBaby_Dec2019.pdf>.

10   Grantly Dick-Read, *Childbirth Without Fear*, Dandelion Digital, 2006.

11   NSW Health, *Breastfeeding Your Baby*, <https://www.health.nsw.gov.au/kidsfamilies/MCFhealth/Publications/breastfeeding-your-baby.pdf>.

12   breastfeeding.asn.au, *Breastfeeding: your questions answered*, <http://breastfeeding.asn.au>.

13   Tiffany Field, Touch Research Institute at the University of Miami Medical School, *Journal of Pediatric Psychology*, vol 24, no 2, 1999.

14   William Sears, *The Baby Book*, Sears Parenting Library, 2013.

15   breastfeeding.asn.au, *Baby Wearing Safety*, <https://www.breastfeeding.asn.au/babywearing-safety>

16   Libby Weaver, *Rushing Woman's Syndrome*, Hay House, 2017.

17   Raymond Arthur, 'Research shows smacking makes chil dren more aggressive and at risk of mental health problems,' *The Conversation*, <https://theconversation.com/research-shows-smacking-makes-children-more-aggressive-and-at-risk-of-mental-health-problems-83394#>

18   Denise Boyd and Helen Bee, *The Developing Child*, 13th edn, Pearson Education, 2013.

19   Gottman Institute, *How to Strengthen Your Child's Emotional Intelligence*, <https://www.gottman.com/blog/strength en-childs-emotional-intelligence/>

20   Mary Sheedy Kurcinka, *Raising Your Spirited Child*, Harper Collins, 2016.

21   Laura Markham, *Peaceful Parent, Happy Kids*, Penguin Ran dom House, 2012.

22   Harvey Karp, *The Happiest Toddler on the Block*, Random House, 2009.

23   aha! parenting, *5 Steps To Nurture Emotional Intelligence in Your Child*, <https://www.ahaparenting.com/parenting-tools/emotional-intelligence/steps-to-encourage>.

24   Sarah Napthali, *Buddhism for Mothers*, Allen & Unwin 2010.

25   Daniel Siegal and Tina Payne Bryson, *The Whole-Brain Child*, Scribe, 2012.

26   Daniel Siegel and Mary Hartzell Med, *Parenting from the Inside Out*, Scribe, 2014.

27   Justin Coulson, *10 Things Every Parent Needs to Know*, ABC Books, 2018.

28   Shefali Tsabury, *The Conscious Parent*, Hodder & Stoughton, 2015.

Index

CPSIA information can be obtained
at www.ICGtesting.com
Printed in the USA
LVHW080618220721
693320LV00009B/163

9 780648 705550